Walking Up Lombard

Walking Up Lombard

- my long journey home -

Reg L. Carver

authorHOUSE®

AuthorHouse™
1663 Liberty Drive
Bloomington, IN 47403
www.authorhouse.com
Phone: 1-800-839-8640

Published by AuthorHouse   06/25/2012

ISBN: 978-1-4772-2823-4 (sc)
ISBN: 978-1-4772-2824-1 (hc)
ISBN: 978-1-4772-2825-8 (e)

Library of Congress Control Number: 2012911286

Also by the Author

Jazz Profiles: The Spirit of the Nineties

with Lenny Bernstein (Billboard Books 1998)

—For Caroline and Chloe—

And for the colorful—the free spirits who dance to songs only they hear—whose dances inspire and leave me longing to hear the same music.

Contents

ACKNOWLEDGMENTS

Many people provided me with inspiration and encouragement to write. (They most likely do not agree with everything I have had to say, but they have supported me in doing something that moves me.) The late Dr. Warren Jacobs, one of my psychiatrists, was the first to suggest I start journaling as a form of therapy. I miss you, Dr. Jacobs, as I know many of your patients do. You were a wonderful man and a great psychiatrist.

Big thanks to my sister-in-law, Jane Gaffey. Our evening discussions on the back porch of Tonic Cottage at Rosemary Beach reminded me that not everyone had given up on me, and also instilled within me the courage to start my blogs. Jane, you may be the kindest person I know.

Thank you to those who read my early blog posts and offered encouraging words, especially Melissa Gaffey, Lauren Moore, and Natalie Gaffey Steadman. Tom Riney understood my need to write from the outset and offered assistance and heartfelt encouragement—peace to you. Thank you to Jim and Janet Murphy for your genuine goodness and for always accepting me unconditionally. Thank you to Mary Riney for being your wise self. One can learn a lot just by observing someone with a good measure of wisdom.

I appreciate others who became regular blog readers and supporters early on. These include my aunt, Pamela Robinson, and my good friend, John Dotson. Blessings to my mother, Shirley Carver, for being the first to read each blog post—and for hitting the "Like" button on *Facebook* for nearly every one! To my mother-in-law, Sue Riney, thanks for your kind and touching words about my writing. (I'm still wearing the beautiful onyx rosary!)

There are so many artists, musicians, writers, and free spirits who have inspired me throughout my life and who have constantly (through their art and souls) reminded me that being and accepting oneself is the highest form of art there is. Specifically, blessings to the spirits of the Buddha, Jesus of Nazareth, Vincent van Gogh, Henri Matisse, Mississippi John Hurt, John Coltrane, Malcolm X, Jimi Hendrix, Bob Marley, Chris McCandless, Bruno Fonseca, and Johnny Cash. Blessings also to Joshua Redman, Bill Frisell, Caio Fonseca, Lenny Kravitz, Rocco DeLuca, JefFREE and Daniel Suelo.

And the biggest thanks of all to my family—my wife, Ann, and our daughters, Caroline and Chloe. Ann, you are the one and only love of my life, my guardian angel, and my guiding light—simply put, you provide meaning to my life. You've encouraged every one of my endeavors—even the craziest ones!—and especially so with this book. In addition to your general encouragement and support, thanks so much for your tireless and masterful editing. Bottom line, this book would never have been written if it weren't for you.

Caroline and Chloe, our beautiful girls (inside and out), thank you for putting up with a moody and, at times, difficult dad. You both are my daily sunshine! (I hope you guys never stop dancing, even if it is simply the dancing that is inside your heart!) I hope you know I wish for you both all the love, joy, and peace in the world. I'm so proud to call you both my daughters—you are both examples of blessings I don't deserve but that somehow God has been so gracious to provide. You have brought nothing but wonder and joy to my life. I wish you could stay my little girls forever—but I know you have growing up to do. You both deserve every good thing that life may bring your way.

And thank you to my sweet beagle, Annabelle. She was right by my side as I wrote every single word. She brought me so much company on so many days I would have otherwise been writing all alone.

One final word of thanks—to all I've ever encountered. I've been blessed in my life to meet young and old, the famous, and, like me, lots of ordinary folk. I've met and spent time with intellects, as well as outcasts and misfits, the conventional and those who took their own path. I've seen you all—yes, every single one of you, I've noticed. I've seen wisdom and I've seen ugly—and just about everything in between. In my own way, I have learned something from everyone I've ever met. My personal mountaintop is wisdom and peace—and if I have made any progress towards the top, it is because of all of you. No one can ever do much all by himself. I hope to reach the top of my mountain some day—and if I do, it will be because each of you will have lent me a hand along the way.

Peace.

RLC

NOTE TO THE READER

This book is part memoir and part collection of thoughts and essays from my blogs, *FindMyOwnCurrent.com* and *fromi2us.com*. (Blog posts are published here as they were on the date noted with minor editing.) Regarding the memoir portions, the events described are recounted to the best of my memory. Conversations may not be recounted verbatim, but they are recitations as I remember them and are an accurate representation of the words and tones conveyed.

All citations to source material and web sites were correct at the time of publication of the original blog posts. However, I cannot state with certainty that such remains the case. I am not responsible for the material of the sources or web sites referenced.

Finally, although I am intimately familiar with generalized anxiety disorder and major depression, I am not a doctor or a psychologist. The contents of this book should not be substituted for appropriate medical treatment.

WE WALKED UP LOMBARD STREET

In January 2008, my wife and I reached our 20th wedding anniversary. To celebrate, we spent several days and nights in San Francisco. We had a ball, cramming in everything we possibly could in that short visit—the wine country of Napa and Sonoma valleys, Haight-Ashbury, fine restaurants, and (my personal favorite) lots of time just walking the streets.

We spent the entire last day just walking. At one point, we found ourselves at the bottom of Lombard Street, known as the "crookedest street in the United States." Lombard runs East-West with a section passing through Russian Hill, where you can find some of the city's (and nation's) most expensive homes. Russian Hill is very steep—even by San Francisco standards. To make it "easier" to traverse, it has eight hairpin turns—this keeps traffic running slowly and safely.

The truth is, the street is actually even steeper than it looks from the bottom. Passing by, Ann says, "hey, this is Lombard. It's the street with all the crazy turns!" (She looked at me as if I should know about Lombard. I didn't.) "Let's walk up," she said, smiling. I shrugged (noticing that everyone else was walking down Lombard), said okay and we started up. Within the first few turns, I was out of breath. Having walked a lot that day already, my flat feet were sore and I realized I had bitten off more than I was sure I could chew.

I huffed and puffed, but we kept walking. I was strengthened by Ann's encouragement. All the way up, the sight of beautiful homes and gardens interrupted my plight. Ann would point out the largest ones and say, "wow, look at that one!" Her encouragement and the scenery were just enough for me to make it to the top. Finally, we looked back down at the quirky beauty that is Lombard Street.

For me, that little trek was the highlight of our trip. And I think Lombard Street is a kind of metaphor for Ann's and my lives together. When we first married, the terrain didn't look so steep. We were full of excitement as we began our journey. But along the way, reality took us into steep twists and turns. Life literally wore me down. But ever the optimist, Ann encouraged me the whole way.

Today, Ann and I are still climbing. And she is still encouraging me to keep climbing the hill that is life. I've always needed Ann. She knows that, too, and has always been there for me. Along life's toughest moments, she has always pointed out a part of its beauty I would have otherwise overlooked. There is no way to ever repay a person to whom you owe your life.

We all need each other. And whether we realize it or not, we may be someone's foundation. We may be the only encouragement that is keeping him or her going. I've learned that the privilege of life carries with it the responsibility to be our best—for our best may be just what saves another's life. Our best just may be what makes another's life worth the walk.

My wife sees me. She sees all of me. She knows what she means to me. And she's never once let me down. She has shouldered many heavy burdens as my angel. She carried the ones I could not carry—and she carried them all with love and grace.

I think Ann probably believes in Heaven. I'm skeptical. But I do know one thing. If Heaven does exist, Ann will live in the Russian Hill section—in a big house with a beautiful garden.

PROLOGUE

"I am seeking. I am striving. I am in it with all my heart."
Vincent van Gogh

The alarms begin their cacophony of bells and tones no later than six o'clock at my home. I hear them all—including my daughters' all the way down the hall. We're a busy bunch, my family. My wife is an executive with a demanding job in a Fortune 100 company. And like their mother, my teenage daughters already have schedules that require constant juggling.

And then there is me. I have no place to go nowadays (I'm winding down my law practice and spend a good bit of time writing, which thankfully, I can do both in my home office). I feel a bit like Thoreau, who once claimed, "for many years I was self-appointed inspector of snow-storms and rain-storms, and I did my duty faithfully." Never mind my status (or lack thereof), the mostly unspoken rule is that I should join the others and rise early. For reasons I begrudgingly admit I do understand, everyone seems in

3

a better mood when we all greet each day (and each other) at the same time—if only for a fleeting moment or two.

Despite the "day break" rule, everyone lets it slide when I sleep in (which is often!). Ann and our girls are very loving and compassionate people. Sometimes I will stay under the covers until 8 or a little after (sometimes fighting early-morning anxiety). I try my best to walk Annabelle (the sweetest and laziest dog on the planet), sort and take my meds, shave, shower, and dress—and still be downstairs by 9.

The truth is, I get no more sleep than anyone else in the family. In fact, I probably get less—for I am quite the night owl. It seems that I never fail to see 2 o'clock—and sometimes I even see 3—illuminated on the nightstand.

I read a lot. Some nights I just lie still and think. (I've always had a lot on my mind.) But my favorite late-night activity is to watch television. I don't usually watch the highly rated talk shows, though. I like the more obscure channels—*Biography, National Geographic, Ovation,* and *Discovery.* I watch the stuff no one else I know seems to watch. These channels offer the most programs on what I have always been most interested in—the lives of extremely creative or unique people—those who march to the beat of their own drum.

In my now 50 years, this is the one constant interest (passion, really) I've carried my entire life. I've always been taken with those who live by their own set of rules—those who think, act, and maybe look a little different from the majority of society. I love studying the lives of geniuses, eccentrics, musicians and visual artists. I love rebels (with or without a cause) and bohemians.

I am not sure I can articulate the "why" of this interest of mine. But I do know that, early on, I felt a restlessness—a kind of pull to somewhere I knew must exist but had never been before. Even as a young boy, I knew I wanted to (had to) escape—from my beginnings, from my anxiety and fears, from just about everything that surrounded me. I knew instinctively that if I did not, I would be resigned to an inevitable life of the mundane. And for me, this was unacceptable.

Czeslaw Milosz, the late Polish poet and prose writer (and winner of the 1980 Nobel Prize in Literature), stated once in an essay (*To Begin Where I Am*) that a writer must summon great courage to tell his story. He noted the writer first had an obligation to acknowledge his current circumstances—his "here." He then must acknowledge that his readers are in some different "here." Bearing in mind the differing perspectives, the writer's duty, according to Milosz, is simply to try to communicate.

Thus, let me begin where I am—my "here" as of now. First off, I am not angry anymore—and anger was my constant mindset for years. Over time, I became angry at almost everything and everyone, it seems. But thankfully, I now hold no ill will towards anything or anyone. (Sadly, I can't say the opposite is true. I did some irreparable damages to certain relationships along my way.) Today, I am at peace—with the world, almost all others, and with myself.

Despite my not having reached the status of being extremely unique or creative, or living the bohemian life, I am at present a very contented—even, I dare say, happy man. I have learned to count my blessings, and I have many. I have a wonderful family whom I love and adore, and from whom I receive much love in return. We all live together in suburban Atlanta in a lovely home with a good measure of creature comforts. I spend my days doing what I love best—thinking and writing. I am afforded the luxury few ever attain—spending the necessary time to contemplate the big questions. I think about lots of things—God, the meaning of a person's existence, the obligations humans have to one another. My career as a writer is beginning to show some promise, and I'm finally taking the time to do something of utmost importance to me—learning to play blues guitar. In short, my life is very good at present.

The preceding paragraph is one I could not have imagined writing just a few years ago. For the truth is, as long as I can remember, I have suffered from generalized anxiety disorder, which ultimately led (in adulthood) to anger and major depression. My unease (or better, *disease*) has always been palpable and deep inside me. Despite the normalcy I managed to project on the outside, my state of mind was anything but normal. For so long, almost every day of my life (literally almost every waking moment), I felt the sensation one has just a second or two before throwing up. Indeed, severe anxiety became such a central part of me that I simply learned early to adapt—this was my "norm."

Beginning in 1999 and for roughly a decade thereafter, my pain and suffering became intolerable. In 2003, I had what only truthfully could be described as a major breakdown. Despite this collapse (and the required medical attention), I continued to try to maintain a stiff upper lip. But, as much as I wanted to, I just could not hold it together as I would have wanted. Ultimately I fell hard and fell far. I nearly lost my marriage, and I lost all my savings and became mired in debt. Along the way, I also lost my self-esteem, my friends, almost all of my pride, and my way. I made a couple of serious suicide attempts. I fell into a deep self-loathing that lasted a very long time. Mostly, I was deeply ashamed of myself and what I had put my family and others through.

But I am one of the very lucky ones. I have been blessed in ways a lot of sufferers of depression never experience. Due to the love, compassion, and absolute and unrelenting support of my wife, and to my discovery of Buddhism, I was given another chance. I know I am very fortunate in this—and I do not intend to blow it this time. I have thought long and hard about my life and what I need to do to gain at least some measure of redemption. I feel I now have at least some of the answers. I want to accomplish a few things with the rest of my life. I want to become the person I should have been all those lost years. I want to be my authentic self—that is, I want to be my own definition of a good person. And I want to do something creative with my life—perhaps involving some combination of writing and music.

Also, I wish to impart my hard-fought wisdom about being oneself to others. I would like to help others who suffer as I have, or who simply want to live a more authentic and happy life. I have been through much turmoil in my life. I have had it all, lost a lot of it, but remain standing and hopeful. Sometimes I wish I had not had to face what I have, but I believe there has been a purpose and value in it all. Hardship has its own blessings. Learning to slay my dragons has brought much peace to my life—a peace I would not have attained without the fight.

I do not have all the answers. Truth is, no one does. But we all carry wisdom of some kind or other. I want to communicate what it means to strive for, and finally be in, my "here"—a place of authenticity, of gratitude, of peace and joy, and a place with love in my heart. This is what motivates me now. This is, in great measure, what makes my life meaningful. With this book, I want to impart some of the valuable lessons I have learned on my journey home—that long journey back home to myself.

BEGINNINGS

"Suffering engenders passion; and while the
prosperous blind themselves, or go to sleep, the
hatred of the unfortunate classes kindles its torch at
some sullen or ill-constituted mind, which is dreaming
in a corner; and sets to work to examine society. The
examination of hatred is a terrible thing."
                                    Victor Hugo, *Les Miserables*

I was born literally in the midst of crisis and turmoil—and it seems
I've been dealing with one crisis or another ever since. By my date
of birth, October 11, 1962, the Cuban and Soviet governments
had already begun building bases in Cuba for nuclear missiles
capable of striking the United States. On October 14, a
United States U2 reconnaissance plane photographed these
bases under construction in Cuba. In the early morning hours of
October 16, National Security Advisor McGeorge Bundy
notified President John F. Kennedy of these photographs.
What became known as the Cuban Missile Crisis was put in
motion, leading the United States and the Soviet Union to the

brink of war. By the end of my first week of life, my fellow citizens and I were on the verge of nuclear annihilation!

The 1960's was a decade of immense turmoil. The United States was undergoing nothing short of an identity crisis. Our country was heavily engaged in the Vietnam War, but its veterans were not embraced by their countrymen—they were treated as pariahs as many were opposed to the United States' involvement. The Civil Rights Movement and hippie movement (including Woodstock) were in full swing. All this revealed way too much intolerance and brought way too much bloodshed. During the first decade of my life, our nation lost President John F. Kennedy, Malcolm X, Martin Luther King, Jr., and U.S. Senator and Presidential candidate Robert F. Kennedy, all to assassination.

Frankly, as a child, a good bit of the time I felt insecure and unsafe. Granted, I have always been a worrier, but I had valid reasons. As I recall, my family always seemed to be dealing with one financial hardship after another. Honestly, I never knew why this was—both my parents were employed full-time as nurses—but it seemed to me that we were constantly struggling to make ends meet.

It's unlikely I will ever understand our situation fully. My mother and I, the only survivors of my immediate childhood family (my father having died in middle age of a heart attack, and my sister succumbing to cancer at age 36), have a code of sorts. It's a silent one, but it has always been there. Each of us has always felt the need to protect the other from the shame of the past. I don't know a lot about hers—and I feel I cannot ask. Likewise, she's never been particularly inquisitive of me. We both know inherently that each has suffered a great deal in our lives. And each of us feels the need to shelter the other as much as we can.

We lived in a marginal house in an equally marginal neighborhood. Everyone's mailbox was held in place by one rusty nail on graying wooden posts. Two things separated the haves and have-nots: gravel or paved driveway, and whether you paid for garbage pick-up or just burned it in a metal barrel. (I guess we were somewhere in the middle—we had gravel, but paid for garbage pickup.) I will never forget the awful stench of burning garbage in the middle of a hot summer.

Like almost all the other kids I knew, I witnessed, and was subjected to, bullying, and verbal and physical abuse (in my case, not by my own family). I had friends who at times had such severely bruised buttocks and legs that I'd wonder if they were ever going to heal. Even the neighborhood pets were not spared—I once found my beloved beagle in front of our house dead from a gunshot wound to the head. There was no need for an explanation. It was simply that there was an abundance of the "wrong kind" in my neighborhood. No one seemed overly concerned with the repugnant happenings in our neighborhood. Our best option was to simply keep our heads down and get along as best we could. I remember always wanting to leave my small hometown of Hopkinsville, Kentucky. And as soon as I was able, I did just that.

Granted, these conditions may not have been enough, on their own, to cause the severe struggles my adulthood would bring. However, I was born with a biological proclivity for a high level of anxiety. My psychiatrists have told me I suffer from an imbalance of chemicals in my brain. I certainly agree with this, and after years of experimenting with many and varied types of treatments and medications, I now take a combination of four medications, which keeps my anxiety to a manageable level.

My degree of suffering has been as much a mystery to me as anyone. Those of us who suffer from mental disorders like anxiety, depression, bipolar disorder, and obsessive-compulsive disorder realize a lot of the time (as in my case) that our pain and suffering are disproportionate to outside stimuli. In other words, we know that many have suffered greater hardships and weathered them better. But, we simply cannot help ourselves—try as we might, we cannot simply "snap out of it." This can be exasperating for loved ones, but our pain is as real as anyone's. And at least thus far, psychiatric treatments have their limitations. Many times, people see only the flaws of those who suffer from mental disorders. But just like anyone else, we are much more than our flaws.

Despite my obstacles to peace of mind, as a child, I did have much going for me. And probably the most important thing was my unbridled curiosity. I discovered books at a very early age. I lived at my local *Walden Books* and the local library. I read only nonfiction—mostly biographies or travel and adventure books. Through these books, I found my first heroes (Martin Luther King, Jr., Malcolm X, JFK, and most of all, a number of artists and musicians), icons whose points of view and way of life were shaping my outlook.

In addition to finding heroes in books, two issues formed a good part of my outlook on life. The first was race relations. I, along with countless other children, was part of busing brought about by the Supreme Court decisions in *Brown v. Board of Education* and *Swann v. Charlotte-Mecklenburg Board of Education*. From the ages of 10 to 13, I attended my small hometown's traditionally all-black elementary and middle schools.

Contrary to what many white folks thought at the time, busing was, for me, one of the greatest blessings of my life. It opened my eyes to the African-American race and its struggles for equality. I also met some of my best childhood pals at these schools. I thrived in this environment. I learned a good bit about black culture—the soulfulness of black folk, their music (especially blues and jazz), and the deep pride African-Americans had in their heritage. As a people, I came to love black folks. To this day, black folks hold a special place in my heart.

The other issue having a lasting—and very negative—impact on me was the Christian faith as taught to me. It would be quite the understatement to say that my family was church-going folk. We belonged to the Second Baptist Church (a part of the Southern Baptist Convention) and we were in our pew practically every time the doors were open. This meant a good six hours of church on Sundays as well as the mid-week Wednesday service.

My father was a deacon in the church. (I never knew what this really meant other than, when elected deacon, folks officially considered you and your family to be "good people.") We learned the way of Christianity through the *King James Version* of the Bible. (In my teens, we all seemed to be buying a Bible known as *The Way*. It was touted as "understandable" and written in modern language. I remember wondering why we never had something like this a long time before!)

Despite all the time I spent in church, I grew to distrust some of what I was taught. I grew more and more skeptical of a lot of what I was learning about God and the Bible. Mostly my skepticism was brought about by what folks claimed to *know*—things folks believed to be certainties, but that even I, a youngster, knew were impossible to actually know.

Please do not misunderstand me. I do believe in the concept of faith. I have a faith in God myself. In fact, I have deep faith about a loving Creator, and I believe in a caring God. But I also feel that God is, in great measure, incomprehensible to man. Unfortunately, my experience was that church leaders (and many ardent followers) claimed to hold intimate knowledge of the details of concepts like Heaven, Hell, and even a holding bin of sorts known as Purgatory. I was subjected to many "fire and brimstone" teachings. I was led to believe that, like Sodom and Gomorrah, I could instantly be turned to ashes for my sins—and there would be literally no end to my suffering!

My learning bits and pieces of the different beliefs of Christians, Jews, and Muslims fueled my skepticism. All three of these largest of the organized religions believed in radically different concepts. But even more troubling to me was that the adherents to each one were convinced the others were wrong in their positions. And, at least from my conservative Baptist upbringing, there was simply no room for error as those I knew saw it.

What I witnessed regarding religion made no sense to me. I became distrustful of those in leadership positions and the majority view on just about anything. I also became fearful of God. All I was witnessing regarding differing points of view about spiritual matters brought me great anguish.

By the time I as ten or twelve years old, I realized that there were many who espoused views with which I simply could not agree. Despite what Southern politicians and others said openly, it was clear to me that no one was superior, or inferior, to another—especially due to skin color. And as to religion, no one was willing to even admit that my questions were valid. It seemed to me that my friends and others readily accepted what was presented as the prevailing views. I did not. I simply didn't fit in.

All the while, I kept reading every bit of non-fiction I could get my hands on. But I did find one hero other than those I read about in books—a man I came to know personally. Although I don't think he would realize it, he played a significant role in my development as a teenager and young adult, and in my choice for a career.

William G. Deatherage, Jr. was (and still is) probably the best lawyer I have ever met. He always struck me as a very proud man and he was absolutely masterful in a courtroom. Beginning as an early teen, I used to love to go to the local courthouse and watch him in action. A former marine who served in the Vietnam War, he did not seem the least bit intimidated by anything or anyone. I was impressed by his intelligence, self-confidence, and courage. Watching Mr. Deatherage in action was what I imagined it would have been like to watch famed lawyer Clarence Darrow.

Along with my fascination with Dr. King and Malcolm X, and my growing desire for justice in the world, watching Mr. Deatherage at work in the courtroom laid the foundation for my wanting to go to law school. I wanted to fight for justice. I felt a strong need to turn conventional thinking on its head. I wanted to right wrongs.

By the age of 15, the idea of law school became an obsession. This, I decided, was my calling. But no one much believed I could ever make it into law school. I had been an average (and sometimes even poor) student at best. Some of this was deliberate on my part. Upon showing up at school for the first day of fourth grade, I was informed that I was skipping the fourth grade and was placed in fifth grade. (This was a complete surprise to me.) I had much potential I was told. I was on the fast track.

But as it turned out, skipping a grade was a nightmare for me. I felt intimidated by the fifth graders and I missed my friends in fourth. I convinced myself the work was too difficult. In an effort to prove it, I started blowing exams. Before long, everyone agreed I was not ready for fifth grade. To my relief, I re-joined my fourth grade class. It seems like a small thing, but it was a turning point, and not a good one. I decided that, from then on, I would make sure I didn't do well enough to be on any fast track ever again. This was the beginning of a pattern of self-sabotage that lasted decades, and to some degree, one with which I continue to struggle to this day.

So, I had done nothing through high school to prove I could get in, much less through, law school. My guidance counselor suggested it was not a reasonable option. I didn't listen to a word of his discouragement. My mind was made up. Upon graduating high school, I enrolled in the local community college (an affiliate of the University of Kentucky). To everyone's surprise, I thrived. I was a motivated student and made great grades.

While I was thriving as a young college student, life at home was falling apart. My parents announced to my sister (who was away at college) and me that they were divorcing. I don't recall being devastated—I just felt kind of numb. As an "adult" myself, it was my decision regarding which parent I would live with. That was an agonizing decision for me. I chose to live with my father—but I've always regretted that. Truth is, my mother needed me. And I've always felt I let her down at a time she needed me most.

For my junior year, I headed to the University's main campus in Lexington. I majored in political science (the traditional major for those wanting to head to law school), and studied a good bit about politics, government, and the criminal justice system. I loved every minute of these years. Not only did I enjoy my classes, but I also loved college life. I loved the freedom. I loved the city of Lexington, Kentucky. I loved how open a college campus is. (I used to go to the "free speech" area and listen to crazy evangelists and others espouse all kinds of opinions and views.) For the most part, everyone was cool with everyone else. I had never witnessed this before, and I loved it.

I applied to the three law schools in Kentucky. (Because of our financial situation, I had to have in-state tuition.) I was accepted to all three. I opted to stay at the University of Kentucky for law school. I had by now met Ann and she would be attending UK as an undergraduate.

I was all set, it seemed. My life was more settled and I was happier than I had ever been in my life. Even my anxiety was at a manageable level—something that had lasted several years by then. I was starting to develop at the least a modicum of self-confidence.

But then one morning I received the most devastating news I had ever received up to that point in my life. I was in UK's main library doing some last minute cramming for an exam. I looked up and saw all three of my roommates headed toward me with shocked looks on their faces. One said, "Reg, Brother Christian (our family's pastor) just called. Your dad died of a heart attack in his sleep last night." Daddy was 46 years old.

I don't know why, but I just instinctively sprang from my chair and started running. I didn't even know where I was going. One of my roommates caught up with me and suggested we take the campus bus back to our apartment. I sat completely silent on the bus ride back.

My father's death left me devastated. All the anxiety and fear returned virtually overnight. I wondered what in the world I was going to do. Would I still get to go to law school? How would I pay for it?

Turns out, while my father was basically insolvent at his death, he did have a pension that allowed my sister and me to receive a total of $600 per month for ten years. She agreed to let me take it for the first three years. I also qualified for grants and a small loan to cover tuition. I stretched the $600 per month to cover my expenses—rent, food, gas, and clothing.

Excepting a few emergencies for which I got help from my sister and my mother, I lived on that budget all through law school. It was very tough. I was never able to buy much at all. There were times I was hungry and had no food.

My law school days were a mix of constant struggle and undying hope. I can best sum up my experience by recalling my feelings one lonely evening I have never forgotten. On this night, I was particularly hungry, and as they say, my cupboards were literally bare. I remember going out to my car and looking under the seats for change. I found 35 cents. Hoping it was enough to buy some sort of snack, I walked one block to a little convenience store. Sure enough, I found I could afford a little package of vanilla sandwich cookies. I made my purchase and I ate them all before getting back to my apartment. I felt very low but proud all at the same time. At least I was working toward my dream of being a lawyer. I couldn't help but laugh at my predicament. I remember thinking, "I might be hungry tonight, but some day I won't have to worry anymore. Some day I will be making a difference in this world, plus have all the money I need."

DISCOVERING OR CREATING?

"Life isn't about finding yourself. Life is about creating yourself."

George Bernard Shaw

I love quotes. With a great quote, so much can be said in only a few words. The quote at the top of this post has made an impact on me for sure. At first I questioned it a bit; now I'm in complete agreement. The difference between "finding yourself" and "creating yourself" is meaningful.

I give a lot of credence to the quote because of its author—George Bernard Shaw—the author of many novels, plays, and essays. Shaw was a genius. He also was a co-founder of the London School of Economics. No doubt, Shaw was a deep thinker and someone I respect greatly.

I have always thought that in being oneself, one simply needed only to peel back all the layers of "stuff" that have been heaped on our hearts and souls through the years—layers of teachings, judgments, criticism, and praise from family, associates, and society—all that may have blinded us as to who we really are. For I believe that, for most of us, we reach adulthood before we really start to question who we really are, what we really believe, and what we want to be and contribute to society. I believed that once this "peeling back" process is complete, our job would be finished and we would have our true self.

But Shaw's quote teaches that I need to add much more to the mix. I believe Shaw would agree with my argument that a peeling back is necessary. It's just that he would take it a step further. I believe Shaw would argue that once the peeling back is accomplished, one would not find a whole person, but merely a kind of shell of potential. Once the peeling is finished, I believe he would say that the real work would just be beginning—that of our starting the proactive business of "creating" ourselves.

The difference in these philosophies is very important. Again, the peeling is only the beginning. There's more work—a lot more work. Once we get to our shell, we can then go about creating most everything about ourselves we want. This goes all the way from our outward appearance, to what we read, to our affiliation or not with a religion, to the friends we choose, to the choice of a spouse or partner, our opinions and views on various issues, and what we choose for a career. This is a lot of creation! And, you know what? It should be, and we should take this work very seriously. We are guaranteed this one life only. We must make the best of it and live as authentically as we can. Otherwise we're simply wasting our time, and others' time as well.

There are many ways to get to yourself—the heart of yourself. The important thing is to do the work that is required of you. You alone know what this entails. You could be like me and require a sort of "peeling back" or "deprogramming" of much of what you have been taught over the years. Or your work may be more in simply beginning the process of creating yourself from the blank canvas with which we all begin. You are probably like most of us—in being yourself, you will have to engage, at least to some degree, in both the "peeling back" and then move to the "creating."

We all can create ourselves in whatever form we choose. The only limitation is that, whatever we create, the creation must be authentic. Otherwise we're not becoming ourselves at all, but just trying to be someone else. We must make sure that, when people look at us, what they see is what they get. We must ensure folks see an accurate picture of us—no exceptions.

There is a real difference between my former philosophy and in Shaw's. As of now, I have adopted Shaw's philosophy as my own and will look more closely at the "creating" part of becoming and being myself.

THE BEAUTIFUL PEOPLE

*"The most beautiful people we have known are those
who have known defeat, known suffering, known
struggle, known loss, and have found their way out
of the depths. These persons have an appreciation,
a sensitivity, and an understanding of life that fills
them with compassion, gentleness, and a deep loving
concern. Beautiful people do not just happen."*
Elizabeth Kubler Ross

I recently ran across this quote and I have thought about it a good bit since. The more I think about it, the more it rings true. Believe me, I do not like to suffer defeat, to know suffering, to know struggle and loss. It was no fun pulling myself from the depths of my depression. But as I look back on it, I am thankful for all I've been through. Like the quote says, I now have more compassion, gentleness, and concern—for others as well as myself.

If you are struggling, please know today that, at some point in the future (hopefully near future), your life will change for the better. And in some strange way that you may not now understand, you will actually realize two things: 1) your troubles made you a better person; and 2) you will be thankful for the mountains you had to climb.

Hold on. Please hold on. You can make it through any hardship placed before you. And, eventually, it will pass, and you will find wisdom as a result.

A BEAUTY IN SIMPLY TRYING

"The truth is that our finest moments are most likely
to occur when we are feeling deeply uncomfortable,
unhappy, or unfulfilled. For it is only in such moments,
propelled by our discomfort, that we are likely to step
out of our ruts and start searching for different ways
or truer answers."

Author Unknown

"May your trails be crooked, winding, lonesome,
dangerous, leading to the most amazing view. May
your mountains rise into and above the clouds."

Edward Abbey

About a dozen or so years ago now, I wrote a book about young jazz musicians (Jazz Profiles: The Spirit of the Nineties, with Lenny Bernstein, Billboard Books, 1998). I profiled 40 rising stars in jazz music, and we included uncut interviews with each one. One theme that ran throughout was that, as much as these artists loved what they were doing, they did not enjoy being on the road so much—not at all.

But there was one exception—a piano player named Benny Green. (He was the sweetest of all those I interviewed—that cat has some soul!) When I asked him about traveling, he said, in part, "there's actually a beauty I think in experiencing the road and experiencing feeling worn out, dealing with some elements that are unexpected and overcoming any kind of obstacle so that when we get on stage, we're able to impart a positive feeling to the listeners .... I think the fact that we've been able to tour and come through these experiences really helps to shape and form the very substance of what we do."

At the time, I thought I understood and could appreciate what Green was saying. But now I know I understand and appreciate it. There is a beauty in struggle. The day-to-day grind of life tests us in ways we don't often realize. It also makes us stronger in the same mysterious ways.

All we can do is try. We'll have good days—and oh, how we love the good days. But don't underestimate the value of the bad ones. They make the good ones sweet, and they impart wisdom. It may sound strange to you, but I now appreciate my bad days. I know they are part of life. I take them as challenges to my character—to what I'm made of.

Wherever you are today, whatever your circumstances, just try. Please just try to do the best you can. As Benny Green says, our challenges are what enable us to impart a positive feeling.

U.S. CIVIL RIGHTS MOVEMENT

The US civil rights movement is something I've always been passionate about. No person can be himself without the freedom to do so. And no person, excepting President Abraham Lincoln, did as much as Rev. Dr. Martin Luther King, Jr. to bring about freedom and equality to black Americans.

I grew up in a small town in Kentucky where blacks were the majority of the population. Black folks were as much a part of my life as whites. I was a part of forced busing beginning in elementary school in the late '60's and early '70's. The school I was sent to, Booker T. Washington Elementary, was just about to fall down—a great contrast to the new Holiday Park Elementary that was 2 miles from my home. But I loved "Booker T." as we called it. I loved that old building—it had character with the old photos of Booker T. Washington, Frederick Douglass, King, and the Kennedys. I loved my fellow students, and I loved the cafeteria ladies. I thrived there.

My best buddies growing up were black and from very poor neighborhoods. Honestly, most of the kids in the entire town were from poor neighborhoods—we just had varied skin tones. As youngsters, we had not learned to notice differences or hate one another. Truthfully, we didn't give desegregation one thought. I don't think I even fully understood why I was bused across town. I just knew I loved that school and the friends I made there.

I really didn't begin to understand much about the depth of black folks' struggles until I moved to Atlanta out of law school. Not long after I moved, I visited the childhood home of Dr. King.

It was there that I got the bug to find out more about the civil rights movement in the Deep South.

I studied a lot about the movement for years—all by reading books. One book that touched me a lot was And The Walls Came Tumbling Down by Rev. Ralph David Abernathy, King's right-hand man in the movement. Abernathy was front and center of the civil rights movement from the beginning. Published in October 1989, I reached out to him. He invited me to his church and we talked a good bit one afternoon about Dr. King, the movement, his own life, many things. Abernathy died shortly after our meeting. I have always been thankful to have met him.

Around this time, my wife got a consulting assignment in Birmingham, Alabama. She would drive from Atlanta to Birmingham on Monday morning and return Thursday evening or Friday. One week I decided to go with her. Each day as she would go off to work, I'd visit historic sites of the movement. In Selma, I traced the route of the march to the Edmund Pettus Bridge. I visited with lawyer J. L. Chestnut, Selma, Alabama's first black lawyer. We talked about the March on Selma—he was there March 7, 1965—Bloody Sunday.

I visited the 16th Street Baptist Church in Birmingham and met with the pastor. He took me to the basement where the four little girls were killed in the Ku Klux Klan's bombing. Little black and white photographs in simple frames hung where they were killed. I went to the jail where King and others were taken at times. There, I spoke with an elderly man—he'd been a janitor and was working one night King was brought in. He told me that the deputies were kind of intimidated by King—"you know, with King being who he was and all."

I traveled to Montgomery (visiting the Capitol, MLK's first church as pastor and the state's archives building) and

Bessemer, a lot of places in Alabama. I just talked to folks about those days. No one seemed offended by my questions, but I did get the sense that most had been asked many of the same questions many times. After visiting those sites, I felt I knew a lot more about the struggle and the pain many endured. I will never understand it totally (you couldn't without being there at the time), but it was very meaningful to me to see and feel these places up close.

One memory sticks out in my mind more than any other. My most vivid memory I have from speaking with Abernathy, Chestnut, and the church pastor was the feeling I always had when the conversations ended. I was touched by how each one seemed to still feel the sting of segregation. Yes, each would agree, a lot of progress had been made, but each man seemed genuinely disappointed that more had not been accomplished in all these years and this disappointment was borne on their faces and in the tone of their speech.

Frankly, I had always been kind of puzzled that those leaders I spoke with did not take more pride in their accomplishments and how far things had come. But, this past Monday, January 17, 2011, I finally understood why. On this day, indeed MLK day, one of the nation's newly elected governors stood before a church congregation and stated that anyone who does not share his Christian beliefs cannot be counted as a "brother or sister." And just who made these statements suggesting inequality regarding religious beliefs? You guessed it, newly elected Governor Robert Bentley of Alabama.

Dr. King, you are now remembered the world over as a giant of men. Indeed, your place among the statues of 20th century martyrs at London's Westminster Abbey and your newly established monument in Washington, D.C. are befitting your stature. But, we miss you here. We wish you could climb down from that wall and monument and walk among us again. You are simply irreplaceable as the conscience of a people. I am happy today that you are free at last. May we all strive to find the same notion of freedom in our hearts and souls.

BUDDHA AND JESUS

I have felt scared and lonely of late. This gets to me. Scared of what? I don't know specifically—just life in general. And I know I'm not really alone—I have family and a few acquaintances—but sometimes I feel very alone. These feelings cause a fair amount of suffering. But I've learned that when I feel these things, I must take refuge—take refuge in something. It is in times like these that I take refuge in the wisdom of two great thinkers—Buddha and Jesus.

I always picture the Buddha with that confident, faint smile on his face—the smile of someone whose wisdom surpasses what mine will ever be. The Buddha's wisdom was gained from putting in hard work of really thinking through life with its myriad of problems. I admire that cat so much. I really would have loved to take him out for dinner one night.

I also think about Jesus of Nazareth. I know of no one who suffered more. Yet he was always concerned with making others feel better. I have a tattoo on my arm of my favorite Bible verse—"Come to me all you who are weary and burdened and I will give you rest." Matthew 11:28. Just thinking about that verse makes me feel better. Jesus is another one I would love to have met. I always picture him with that long hair and in those worn sandals—he was always walking, it seems. I've always thought he would have been more laid back than portrayed in the Bible. I mean, look at whom he hung with—a lot of times the outcasts—the ones nobody cared to listen to or be with. If Jesus were here today and living in NYC, I believe he'd have a place in the East Village. If he were on the West coast, I'm pretty sure he'd be rocking his

31

Birkenstocks on the corner of Haight and Ashbury—just talking about things.

All this got me thinking about a book I have on the similarities between Buddha and Jesus—Jesus and Buddha: The Parallel Sayings, edited by Marcus Borg and Ray Riegert. Jesus and Buddha lived years and cultures apart, yet they were alike in so many ways. Both were rebels for their times and places. Both suffered greatly in their search for truth. Both faced much loneliness, yet spent much time instructing and inspiring others—both so selfless. The parallel sayings and thoughts revealed in the book inspire awe.

Tonight after work I will pull the book from the shelf and begin re-reading it. I will take refuge in the writings and thoughts of these two. I will be more enlightened about Christianity and Buddhism and I will feel less lonely. Sometimes it's just the small things—but when you find yourself lonely, as I said, take refuge in something—something positive. Before you know it, the world won't seem like such a lonely place.

I MISS MY DAD

My father, Bobby Carver (1937-1984), was born into a farming family in Rosewood, Kentucky. The youngest of twelve children, he lost his mother at age 2 and his father when he was 15. Upon his mother's death, he was groomed to take on his mother's household chores. From the time he was just a kid until he left home after high school, he was put in charge of maintaining the home—cooking, cleaning, washing clothes, etc. His father, Otis, and older brothers and sisters, ran the farm—working fields, harvesting crops, taking care of livestock and other animals—all the never-ending chores that went into maintaining a farm. As difficult a life as this was for a child, my dad always said he got the better end of the bargain. I remember him saying, "Working the fields was hard. My chores were endless, but at least I was indoors and could find a way to stay cool in the summer and warm in the winter."

Upon graduating from Dunmor High School's class of 1955, he moved to Hopkinsville, and took a job at Western State Hospital (a public asylum for the mentally ill) and pursued a degree in nursing. He did become a nurse and remained at Western State the remainder of his life, eventually becoming an administrator there in staff development. While in nursing school, he met my mother. They married January 25, 1958, and had a daughter, Sheila (1959-1996), and me in 1962.

To skip ahead, my dad (I called him Pops) died unexpectedly of a heart attack at age 46. I was 21 at the time, a senior in college. Pops just died in his sleep. My dad meant the world to me. Since that time, I've had to rely on memories of him.

But I have great and plentiful memories. For one, I will remember him as the hardest working man I've ever known. In addition to his full-time job at Western State Hospital, to make ends meet, he worked the evening or overnight shift at a local nursing home. This was also full-time. I honestly don't know when the man slept. I do remember him catching naps when he could. (At his funeral, our pastor told me it really was no surprise he died such a young man. He said to me, "Reg, it's no wonder your dad died so young. He crammed a life's worth of work into 46 years. Your dad was simply worn out.") My father did what he had to do for his family.

Another memory of him is his generosity with his time. Pops could simply not say no to anybody—especially if it involved doing something for kids. He was involved with all my baseball teams from the time I was 5 to 15. He was always active at our schools, spending time running concession stands at football and basketball games. He worked numerous fundraisers for the high school band program. At Christmastime, we were always taking gifts to kids who would otherwise get nothing for Christmas. (I admired him for this, but I remember wanting some of those gifts he gave away to other kids! I've never been as generous as my dad.) Simply put, Pops was always busy helping somebody with something.

I remember that Pops was a religious man. He served as a Deacon at the Second Baptist Church and taught Sunday school to the Young Married Couples class. (We were at church every time the door was open, it seemed. Literally whole Sundays were spent at church. I remember not liking this at all!) I've heard enough of those Southern Baptist sermons to last a lifetime. If I had to, I could probably preach a Southern revival off the cuff!

The two things I remember most about Pops and his religious beliefs were—a) his favorite Bible verse—"But my God shall supply all your need according to His riches in glory by Christ Jesus." Philippians 4:19, and—b) he constantly told me that my sins of omission would always be greater than my sins of commission. (I never really knew what this meant until I was an adult. But my father rarely disciplined me for something I had done wrong. He would just say that he knew that I knew what I did was wrong and I could just think about it for a while. Then he'd go through his spiel about the omission/commission thing. Again, at the time it was all over my head. But I did hate to disappoint him. He was right, just thinking about what I had done was usually plenty of punishment for me.)

My dad was a great Southern cook. I remember lots of fried meats—especially pork and chicken. We also had lots of vegetables at meal time—tomatoes, potatoes, all kinds of beans, including black-eyed peas, pinto beans, and green beans. Homemade biscuits and cornbread were my favorite. During Thanksgiving and Christmas, he always made chocolate and peanut butter fudge. What I would give for some of that peanut butter fudge now!

My most vivid and lasting memories of my dad, however, are of his love and his spirit. Pops had a hard life in many ways. (He rarely talked to me about his childhood, but once he told me that he was extremely lonely as a child.) But Pops was always in a good mood—always trying to make others feel good or in good spirits. He was a great mimic and could have me in stitches impersonating quirky folks we all knew.

I mostly just miss being with my dad. He loved me and told me so often. I loved him, too, and loved spending time with him. He could make anything fun and I miss his silliness. He made me feel safe. I miss being near him. I wish that I could have introduced him to Ann and our girls. He would have loved and admired Ann a lot, I know. And he would have adored our daughters—oh my gosh. He would have been a wonderful grandfather.

I wish I had just one more day with him. Sometimes, I think that's about all I really need. I could tell him about my lost years and he would let me hear his thoughts. Sometimes I think that if we had just one more day together, everything would be okay again.

INSPIRATIONAL LIVES

"All my life I had been looking for something, and
everywhere I turned someone tried to tell me what it
was. I accepted their answers too, though they were
often in contradiction and even self-contradictory.
I was naïve. I was looking for myself and asking
everyone except myself questions which I, and only
I, could answer. It took me a long time and much
painful boomeranging of my expectations to achieve a
realization everyone else appears to have been born
with: that I am nobody but myself."
Ralph Ellison, *Battle Royale*

I am fascinated with creativity. To me, to create something—a
work of art, a song, a hairstyle, anything—no one else has done
is about the coolest thing there is. So I guess this explains my
fascination with people. Each one of us is a unique creation in
two ways—1) there will never be another of any of us, and 2) we
each carry a story that is truly our own and no one else's.

My fascination with individuals has been with me my entire life, but it has evolved greatly over time. As a youngster, I was chiefly concerned with the stories of those I considered "of consequence." (This is the term I used silently in my own head.) In my immature mind, only those known the world over (Gandhi, Abraham Lincoln, JFK, MLK, Albert Einstein, Picasso, van Gogh, Elvis Presley—you get the picture) were worthy of my attention. I considered everyone else to be swimming in a gigantic pool of mediocrity. And I thought of myself as no different. By the time I was a teenager, I had such low self-esteem that I felt I was not only in that pool, but was clearly in the deep end. I viewed my life as a daily grind of treading water. In my view, life was a constant struggle of getting nowhere.

As ignorant and callous as I was on the one hand, I also had a tender place in my heart for those whom I considered to be living against seemingly impossible odds. I felt extreme compassion for the poor, the very ill, for those with disabilities. I was especially concerned about children who felt unloved, or were mistreated by their parents. (I was blessed with loving parents. I know I would not have made it in some of the households of some of the kids I knew.)

My interest in these two factions of society was a major factor in my becoming a lawyer. With my twisted and increasingly elitist points of view, it seemed like the most logical choice. By becoming a renowned lawyer, I could reach my goal of becoming a person of consequence, all the while fighting for justice for the ones who most needed help. Indeed, it was a grand plan, and one I held onto through my law school days.

It has taken many years for me to realize the simple truth that every single person has value—and equal value. Obviously there are those with an abundance of talent in some area or other.

There are those with unusual drive or ambition. And, no doubt, there are some that are just plain lazy or are simply unconcerned with the values of the mainstream. But all of us are people of consequence. Each of us impacts (for good or otherwise) everyone we encounter. Sometimes the impact can be truly inspiring.

My fascination with people is as strong as ever. (I hope it never goes away!) But now my fascination extends to folks of all walks of life. We are more alike than we are different. As the Dalai Lama often says in his still-evolving English, "we are all same." I've learned that everyone experiences challenges in life. As a result, everyone has triumphs, failures and tragedies. All these bring chances to teach and to learn.

THE GENIUS OF DAVID FOSTER WALLACE

I really don't believe in coincidences anymore. The older I get, the more I see (or at least I think I see) that nearly every event of consequence in my life is somehow related in time and context to others. Now this is obviously just my personal opinion and is based upon nothing more than my own feelings and experiences. Nevertheless, I feel strongly about this and, at least for the foreseeable future, I'm holding tightly to this line of thinking.

One example of a "non-coincidental coincidence" started taking shape one recent Friday evening. On very short notice, my wife decided to visit her sister in Colorado over the Labor Day weekend. A great and fun opportunity for her, but I miss her terribly and feel very lonely when she's gone. So, to combat these feelings, I hit the local Barnes & Noble seeking a good book to keep me occupied.

I hit the jackpot! There it was—just sitting pretty on the New Biographies shelf, Although Of Course You End Up Becoming Yourself, the long-anticipated chronicle of journalist David Lipsky's five days spent with the late writer David Foster Wallace on Wallace's Infinite Jest book tour. DFW is hands down my favorite writer. But he's also much more than that—he is a hero of mine. With the publication of Lipsky's book, I not only now have the opportunity to get inside the head of a man I so admire, but it sparked the idea for this blog post. All "coincidence"—I think not!

41

David Foster Wallace was a literary genius. Indeed TIME rated Infinite Jest as one of the top 100 novels of all time (covering the period of 1923 to the present). Moreover, while still in his 30's, Wallace received the John D. and Catherine T. MacArthur Foundation Award, the only prize granted to someone for simply being a "genius."

But as admired as DFW is for his fiction, it is his non-fiction that truly speaks to me. A Supposedly Fun Thing I'll Never Do Again and Consider The Lobster are two of my favorites. (Both are absolutely hilarious!)

But it is his This Is Water that is the most meaningful to me. This little book displays Wallace's true genius—not the literary kind (well, all his work displays the literary kind), but his genius in simply knowing what is important in life and what one should be thinking about literally on a daily basis.

This Is Water is the publication of Wallace's 2005 commencement speech at Kenyon College in Gambier, Ohio. It takes about 20 to 30 minutes to read, but is so full of wisdom that it has the capacity to make you vow to be a better person. In sum, Wallace suggests to each of us that each and every day we're given a choice—a freedom—as to how to approach that day. We can do it through a "natural, hard-wired, default setting which is to be deeply and literally self-centered and to see and interpret everything through the lens of self," or we can exercise real freedom—"[t]he really important kind of freedom [that] involves attention and awareness and discipline, and being able truly to care about other people and to sacrifice for them over and over in myriad petty, unsexy ways every day." "That," he says, "is real freedom."

And this, I submit, is the real genius of David Foster Wallace. Clearly he will be remembered as a literary giant. There will be (probably already are) college courses devoted to the study of his writing. And I believe this to be important and an honor Wallace deserves. But I will remember David Foster Wallace mostly for being a genuinely kind and thoughtful human being. Do yourself a favor and read This Is Water. You deserve to be reminded now and again of the lessons Wallace imparts.

ASK YOURSELF THESE THINGS

I've just finished the new memoir from Liz Murray entitled Breaking Night. It tells the incredible and inspiring story of Ms. Murray's life journey from a severely impoverished childhood in the Bronx to her rise to attending and graduating from Harvard University in 2009. Granted, many folks who grow up disadvantaged go on to Ivy League schools and lead productive and successful lives. But Ms. Murray's story is unique, and portrays in heartbreaking detail the perseverance of a child in the face of overwhelming obstacles.

From her earliest memories, Ms. Murray was the victim of severe neglect, drug-addicted parents, squalid living conditions, malnutrition and hunger, and deep loneliness. Taken from her parents, she was placed briefly in a cold and uncaring group home setting, eventually choosing to escape and live on the streets. By her teens, she had lost her mother to AIDS and her father to life in a homeless shelter.

As a young teen, she endured years of day-to-day survival, essentially as a wanderer. Nights were spent in and on subways, stairwells, rooftops, with intermittent stays at friends' houses. Attending school only sporadically, her days were spent literally just trying to make it hour by hour—her goals being safety, warmth, and avoiding the pain of hunger.

After years on the streets, at 17, Ms. Murray was literally on the brink of collapse—collapse of body and spirit. I think it's safe to say that most of us would not have made it. Under like circumstances, most of us would say our lives were going to go nowhere and we would simply give up.

However, at the lowest and most critical of times, Ms. Murray asked herself a simple question that set her on a path of change. Says Murray, "I was inspired by a question that kept repeating itself in my mind: Could I really change my life? I'd spent so many days, weeks, months, and years thinking about doing things with my life, and now I wanted to know, if I committed to a goal and woke up every single day working hard at it, could I change my life?"

This question focused Ms. Murray. She found a high school willing to accept her, graduated with straight A's (cramming four years of work into two), and managed to obtain a scholarship to Harvard from The New York Times. While in college, she started a company called Manifest Living, which provides workshops to inspire folks to achieve their dreams.

At the end of the book, Ms. Murray reveals what she considers the most important lesson of her life. Says Murray, "marveling at one thing I know for sure: homeless person or business person, doctor or teacher, whatever your background may be, the same holds true for each of us: life takes on the meaning you give it."

This brief post cannot in any way capture the beauty and lessons described in Breaking Night. It cannot recount the hardships she endured and the heartbreaking and demeaning aspects of her life on a daily basis. I highly recommend that you read this book to capture her full story. But I can tell you that this book is a testament to the best of the human spirit. I know I am not a strong enough person to have endured what Ms. Murray endured in her life. But her spirit has strengthened mine.

I ask you to ask yourself the questions Ms. Murray asked herself—a) if I commit to a goal and work hard toward it every day, can I change my life?, and b) what meaning does life hold for me? If you ask yourself these questions and then honestly work toward the change you wish for yourself, I believe you will find yourself on the way to self-discovery and a measure of fulfillment.

I've made a personal commitment to change myself. I have not yet worked as hard as Ms. Murray toward my goals, but I am headed in the right direction. You will find the same can be true for you as well. For more information, go to www.manifestliving.com.

ROCCO DELUCA–THE ETHEREAL ARTIST

One of the greatest thrills in life for me is to discover a truly unique individual. And I'm all the more excited when the person happens to be an artist of some kind—whether a musician, visual artist or writer. I can't really explain the reason for my exuberance on these occasions—I only know that I feel completely alive when I am experiencing their art, for example, attending a live concert. Sometimes, these are life-changing moments for me.

In my humble opinion, one of the greatest musicians I've ever encountered is the blues/rock musician and vocalist Rocco DeLuca. A young cat (b. December 27, 1975) with an old soul, DeLuca's literally been steeped in music his entire life. (DeLuca's father was the touring guitarist for Bo Diddley. He talks of his dad's and uncles' late night jam sessions when, as a toddler, DeLuca would curl up inside the bass drum and fall asleep to the thumping of the blues.)

Rocco DeLuca plays a resonator guitar in both "fingerpicking" and "slide" styles which produces a kind of haunting blues sound that captures the essence and a combination of blues legends like Robert Johnson, Mississippi John Hurt, John Mayall, and John Lee Hooker—all with more intensity. He's also an accomplished vocalist with a voice unlike any I've ever heard. His vocals are visceral, aggressive, sweet, mysterious, and absolutely piercing—all at the same time. He comes by this sound honestly, once saying, "[y]ou've gotta die a few times and be fierce enough to fall. I've fallen on my face many times. Whether it was on stage or with my family, but's it's those times and battle scars that make my music what it is today."

DeLuca has released two full-length CD's, 2006's I Trust You To Kill Me, and 2009's Mercy.* He has toured worldwide with his 1931 National guitar and continues a regular touring schedule.

The music of Rocco DeLuca is literally like nothing I've ever heard—it's serious music and simply hauntingly beautiful. Watching him live in concert is the most moving of treats. His intensity and stage presence are unrivaled. One leaves the concert with the feeling you've just witnessed someone bare his soul completely—much like fans used to describe the experience of witnessing John Coltrane at work.

I struggle for words to describe Rocco DeLuca and his sound. Please check out his music. And if you ever have the chance to catch him live, then you will grasp what I'm trying to say. I promise you that. Rocco DeLuca is an artist and musical genius in every (and in the very best) sense of the words.

The quotations used in this post were taken from www.artistdirect.com/artist/bio/rocco-deluca/355078

*Since this original blog post, DeLuca has issued another full-length album, 2012's Drugs 'N Hymns. I recently attended his latest Atlanta gig. I got to the venue early. To my surprise, as I approached the venue, I saw Rocco—standing by himself on the sidewalk—just people watching. I introduced myself and tried my best to explain how much he means to me. He was as gracious as I had imagined he would be. It was a blessed evening for me.

ANNE MAHLUM–BACK ON MY FEET

Anne Mahlum is a runner. And she's a runner with a purpose. She's the founder and president of Back On My Feet, a nonprofit organization whose mission is to promote "self-sufficiency of homeless populations by engaging them in running as a means to build confidence, strength and self-esteem."

This whole story began while Anne was a teenager. Her relationship with her father, whom she loves dearly, made for difficult times. Her father's drug, alcohol and gambling addictions troubled her deeply and she sought solace in running. Anne ran "a lot," she says, "to save myself from the despair."

A few years ago, Anne's daily route led her past a Philadelphia homeless shelter. She noticed a group of guys outside the shelter, on the corner. They reminded her of her dad, she says, and because so, she was drawn to them. Says Anne, "I wanted to share this sport with these guys in hopes they would reap the same benefits I did—better self-esteem, confidence and discipline."

The running club took hold, and it became much more. In July 2007, Anne founded Back On My Feet. In its mission statement, BOMF notes that "our organization consists of much more than just running: our members participate in a comprehensive program that offers connections to job training, employment and housing." Ms. Mahlum believes that "the only way for real change to happen in someone's life is for that person to voluntarily participate in making those changes." Anne reminds us that many programs try and force people to do things, "but when does forcing anyone to do anything ever have long-lasting sustainable results?" Accordingly, with BOMF, benefits to club members are earned by maintaining 90 percent attendance at morning runs three days per week.

Currently BOMF has chapters in Philadelphia, Baltimore, Washington, D.C., Boston, and Chicago. In 2011, it expanded to Dallas-Fort Worth, Atlanta, and Minneapolis. To date the organization has more than 400 active members and has assisted almost 450 individuals find a better way of life.

In 2008, Anne Mahlum was named a Top 10 CNN Hero. For what it's worth, she's one of mine as well. The world is a better place because of people like Anne Mahlum. To learn more about BOMF, please visit www.backonmyfeet.org.

The quotations from this post were taken from www.cnn.com/2010/OPINION/11/18/mahlum.hero.rescue/index and www.backonmyfeet.org.

THE MEEK ARE OUR ANGELS

"Sometimes an angel is a tattooed cook in a shop
window who smiles and waves as you walk by."
(Tweet by @HumanBeam)

I follow @HumanBeam on Twitter. She posted this a couple days ago. I remember reading it and thinking about how right she is. I then started to think about all the folks I encounter every day who are angels. And I also started thinking about public figures who are angels. I've decided all angels have the following in common—all angels are meek and also are servants to their fellow man.

I think about this sort of thing a lot—always have. I've always been drawn to those who are the servants, the working class, the outcasts and homeless. I'm so drawn to these folks that I have been accused many times as being somewhat weird or that my attachment to the "little people" or those who live on the fringe is somehow abnormal or even in fact harmful to my own self-esteem or me.

But I think that, in truth, I just love to see angels. And I seem to find them most often, as I've said, in the meek and in those who serve. Dictionary.com uses words like "humbly patient," "gentle," and "kind" to describe the meek. So, to me, being attracted to the meek is not strange at all.

Think about it for a minute—whom do you know that you would classify as an angel? If you answer honestly, I bet it would be someone meek and who answers or has answered a call to serve. Perhaps it's someone well known like Mother Teresa or Gandhi—or perhaps it's someone you encounter regularly like your own mother, a person who looks after a loved one for you, or the bagel shop worker who knows just how much cream cheese you like. I would bet it's not a Fortune 500 CEO, a professional athlete, a celebrity, or a member of royalty. As a society, we hold these folks up as giants—persons to revere. We long to be like the rich and live in gated communities and send our children to private schools—we try to steer clear of the "little people." But, you see, if you look at it honestly, you will find that our real angels are the ones we so often forget.

The angels are the ones who make our lives work. The servants make life easier for the rest of us. But often times, we don't embrace them as we should. We treat them as outcasts and we don't befriend them or invite them into our homes. We keep the angels at a distance. As @HumanBeam says, sometimes our angels look a little different. Sometimes they don't have as much as others. Some of us worry about maintaining a certain image, and inviting the meek into our lives just wouldn't do.

My friends, let's not forget about our angels. As a matter of fact, I would suggest that we all strive to be a little more meek ourselves. As Jesus pointed out, it's the meek who shall inherit the Earth.

There was a time in my life when I wanted to be someone whom society revered. But as I get on in age, I just want to be meek. It's a lofty goal, indeed, but I wish to dare to become an angel. And I don't think there's anything strange about that all.

GIVERS AND TAKERS

"It is more blessed to give than to receive."
Bible, Acts 20:35 (KJV)

"Act with kindness, but do not expect gratitude."
Confucius

Today's post is short and simple, but for me at least, it packs a powerful message and reminder for us all.

In my opinion, there are simply two types of people in this world—givers and takers. We all have traits of both at times and I believe we can and often do even change from one to the other on occasion. But, as I see it, by and large, our default setting is either as one or the other. I also believe each of us knows into which category we fall.

If you know me personally, you know that I am a taker. I am embarrassed to admit this, but it's just the truth. In my lifetime, I have done far more taking than giving.

If you are a giver, God bless you! I want to take time out today to say thank you. I believe that not enough of you sense that others acknowledge you to be a giver. This is a shame. The givers probably aren't told "thank you" enough by us takers. But I do want the givers to rest assured that we takers do recognize you and, though we might not say it often enough (or at all), we are extremely grateful to you.

I don't quite know how I'm going to do it, but I wish to change my default setting. I know it will be a long road because changing a basic personality trait has to be one of the most challenging tasks one can pursue. But I don't think it's impossible.

Starting today, I'm going to be all eyes and ears when it comes to folks I know who are givers. I'm watching and listening to their every move. I want to emulate givers as much as possible—with the hope that, one day, I, as well as those who know me, will be able to say I've done what it takes to be moved to the givers category.

This movement would be one of my greatest accomplishments in life. And it would simply mean the world to me. I may not get there, but I am going to try.

WE NEED BOB MARLEY

"Every man gotta right to decide his own destiny."
Bob Marley

I love Bob Marley. I love his music. I love his dreadlocks. I love his Jamaican accent and vernacular. Most of all, I love Bob Marley's smile and what was his outlook on life. For the last ten or so years, I have carried a picture of him in my pocket everywhere I go—yes, that's the truth! When I look at that picture, I believe everything will be alright. He left this world way too soon.

Ann and I have a friend with deep Jamaican roots. When we get together with him and his family, we play reggae music and talk a lot about Jamaica and Marley. This past Saturday evening, we had dinner at his family's home. They cooked a traditional Jamaican meal—chicken, rice, plantains and pineapple upside down cake. We capped the evening with a little Jamaican rum. What a wonderful meal and evening!

At one point, my friend asked his daughter to go down to the basement and get something for him. She came up with a framed promotional poster (an original, not a copy) from Marley's 1979 album, Survival. The theme of this particular album is African unity—the album cover contains the flags of nearly all African countries at the time and the album itself also contains the hit song, Africa Unite.

My friend told me that he and his wife bought the poster and had it framed as a gift for me. I was blown away. It is beautiful with a great shot of Marley front and center. (I already have it hanging prominently in my office.) I was very touched by my friend's and his wife's generosity and I was even more touched that they knew of my love for Marley and wanted to do something so special for me.

As I studied the album cover, I thought about the irony of the events unfolding in Egypt and Libya. I thought about how deeply Marley cared about his people in Jamaica but also in what he considered his Mother Land, Africa. He would be deeply saddened at the state of Africa today—the oppression, the violence, the starvation.

The quote of Marley's at the beginning of this post is something he believed in to his core. The oppression of a people (especially by its own leader) would shock and sadden Marley greatly. It should shock and sadden us all, really. Oppression of another person in any form is evil. No person can discover and be himself or herself without the freedom to do so. With the exception of prayer, there may be little that most of us can do to stop the oppression that is going on in Africa right now. We must depend on world leaders and the UN to deal with these situations.

But oppression comes in many forms and we can do something about some of these forms. How often do we engage in the act of oppression of another just by our judgments and criticism? We must guard ourselves against oppression of another human being. The psychological and emotional scars from oppression can be everlasting. We must be tolerant of our fellow man and we must never stifle one's dreams or destiny in any way. We each owe it to our brothers and sisters to lift them up and not attempt to hold them down.

As Marley says, everyone has the right to decide his own destiny. Please don't trample on anyone's right to do that. I'm reminded of an oft-repeated quote from the Dalai Lama. Says he, "it is necessary to help others, not only in our prayers, but in our daily lives. If we find we cannot help others, the least we can do is to not harm them."

Please, let us all pledge to let our brothers and sisters be. Let's pledge to let them decide their own destiny—in Africa, yes, and all over the world. We can start in our own life, in the lives of our family members, and in our own community. Please, let's stop harming one another through oppression.

BROTHER MALCOLM

"There is no better than adversity. Every defeat, every heartbreak, every loss, contains its own seed, its own lesson on how to improve your performance the next time."

Malcolm X

My mind is filled constantly these days with thoughts regarding positive change, wisdom, enlightenment and redemption. For inspiration and guidance, I look to others who so wholly transformed themselves that one could argue they actually changed from one person to another. I study these folks and I know it can be done.

I so want to change for the better—in all ways. And I work at it almost each and every moment I can muster. I feel that so few people really see me and see a transformation. It's so frustrating that I want to scream it from a mountaintop that I'm trying! But I know I am still far from perfect. I still carry pride, insecurities, weakness and fear—all these traits took up residence inside me long ago. I also know people really do see one's heart. If and when a true and complete transformation is within me, it will one day be revealed. And not only will I not have to scream it, I won't have to utter even the faintest of whispers.

Malcolm X. Just let the name be uttered and folks will have some sort of visceral reaction. I mean everybody. Some years ago, I was asked to speak to various middle schools about he US Civil Rights Movement. (The schools were celebrating "Law Day" and local lawyers were asked to speak on the topic.) I treasured the opportunity. I would walk these kids through the milestones—the US Supreme Court decisions in Plessy v. Ferguson (in 1896 upholding that "separate but equal" facilities was valid under the US Constitution), and then the 1954 decision in Brown v. Board of Education (where the Court reversed itself and declared segregation to be a violation of our most supreme law.)

I would discuss the roles of Thurgood Marshall and Martin Luther King, Jr. (By this point, the kids had long lost interest and were fidgeting.) But I always saved the role of Malcolm X for last. Inevitably the black children would perk up. I'd ask if anyone knew his most famous slogan. Hands would shoot up and several would shout, "by any means necessary!" The black kids loved Malcolm X. The white kids sat still with uncomfortable looks on their faces. Sometimes, teachers would start to give me a look that said, "please don't incite these kids!"

Malcolm X has been totally misunderstood by most. Society still views him as one who preached racism and black supremacy. Many remember that he at one time referred to white folks as "devils." All this is true, of course. But what folks do not recall is Malcolm X's complete transformation.

Malcolm X was a criminal at one time. He spent time in prison. While locked in a cage, he educated himself and became a Muslim. He devoted himself to the Nation of Islam and for years was its chief spokesman. Through it all, Malcolm X believed in himself and believed that what he spoke was the truth. He never espoused views he didn't wholeheartedly believe and he was always his own man. (Unlike so many leaders, he never sold out. He could not be bought.)

And so it was that in the last year of his life, he came to see that Elijah Muhammad, the head of the Nation of Islam, did not stand for the truth as Malcolm X saw it. In March 1964, he formally broke from the Nation of Islam. Remaining a Muslim, however, in April of the same year he made his pilgrimage to Mecca in Saudi Arabia. He completed the Hajj (the religious duty for Muslims as a demonstration of the solidarity of the Muslim people and their submission to Allah—God in the Arabic language.) It was during this trip that Malcolm X's transformation was completed. He became a Sunni Muslim and witnessed people of all races interacting as equals. His mind was convinced of this truth and he spoke of this truth, noting, "I believe in human beings, and that all human beings should be respected as such, regardless of their color."

Malcolm X returned from Saudi Arabia a changed man. Sadly, we never got to witness the fruition of his transformation. From the time of his split with the Nation of Islam, he lived only 11 months. He was assassinated February 21, 1965 while speaking in Manhattan's Audubon Ballroom.

The death of Malcolm X was a terrible loss for the US and the world. I believe, if given the chance, he would have stood as a giant for equal rights for all. Indeed, like so many who dared to speak the truth as he saw it, cowards silenced Malcolm X. There is no more cowardly act than to destroy one who stands for truth.

I am thankful today for the lessons of Malcolm X. He has taught me that one—anyone—can go from a mindset of pain and anger to love and respect for all. Total transformation can take place in any human being. This, I believe, is Malcolm X's greatest legacy. Despite his earliest thoughts and speeches, he eventually discovered reality. As always, he stood up for his beliefs. He stood for truth, as he understood it at the price of his life.

Brother Malcolm, may you rest in peace. I know of your transformation, and you are a treasure to me. I pray for strength such as yours in my continued journey.

Sources for this post include Malcolm X: A Life Of Reinvention, *by Manning Marable.*

RAGE AGAINST ANY MACHINE

"Fear is the path to the dark side. Fear leads to anger. Anger leads to hate. Hate leads to suffering."
Yoda—Fictional character from George Lucas's *Star Wars*

As I understand it, the medical community does not fully understand the causes of depression. Just like cancer, doctors have ideas as to some of the causes, but it gets very complicated very quickly. For what it's worth, I believe there are too many causes of depression to count. And I know that, for me personally, my depression is rooted in a) a generalized anxiety disorder, b) fear of the impending Horrible Thing (which I define as something unknown that will be so catastrophic to me that I won't be able to survive it), and c) a good measure of pure, unadulterated rage.

The anxiety and fear have been with me as long as I can remember. The anger was brought to a slow and steady boil over the course of many years. My anger became directed (justifiably so or not) at three distinct "machines"—the legal profession, the field of psychiatric treatment and well, myself.

Rather than simply learning to turn down the burner, my controls became stuck on high. My anger boiled until it evaporated completely. I'm thankful it's now gone (for the most part—all that is left are lingering vapors), but before leaving me, things became very ugly at times—inside and outside of me, and in the destruction of many personal relationships, some of which I have salvaged, some not. I did a lot of damage over the course of several years. For what it's worth, I am no longer angry at the "machines" mentioned above, but in years of immaturity and depression, I blamed a good many of my problems on them. (As for myself, I still blame a lot on myself.) But, I'm here to tell the truth—ugly or not.

With respect to my becoming a lawyer, I started compromising my principles very early on. As a matter of fact, before I had even graduated from law school, I already was looking to money as a path to security, which I thought would ultimately lead me to happiness. Because of money, I had sold my principles of seeking to right wrongs and demanding justice before even receiving my cap and gown.

I did well in law school. The summer between my 2nd and 3rd years, I landed a clerkship with a prestigious law firm in Atlanta. It was there that I got a taste of the good life. And, oh, how I loved the good life. I saw that a law degree could lead to a good position with a good law firm. And a good position with a good law firm could lead to riches I was not used to—plenty of spending money, a nice car, quality clothes, fine dining (overnight I went from those vanilla sandwich cookies to duck confit!), even a nice house in a nice neighborhood—all the things I never had growing up. I was completely swept up by all this. It was only later that I discovered at what price it would all come.

That summer convinced me that I had it made. As an overpaid law clerk (who knew virtually nothing about practicing law), I received $550 per week for the summer weeks of June through August of 1986. (At the time, this was all the money in the world to me.)

Basically, the summer clerkship was one long interview. The summer clerks were paid to do nothing more than show up at the office and prove we could look nice and make nice before clients. Occasionally we were given a research assignment to make it look as though we were being paid for something more than an extended interview.

Despite the relaxed atmosphere, I worked my ass off that summer. I took on every project I could get my hands on. I even worked Saturdays and Sundays. When not swamped, I would ask partners for more work. I wanted all to know I was willing to do anything for a good job. I worked to the point of making the other clerks uncomfortable. There was nothing I wouldn't do for a full-time position as an associate lawyer in this firm. The partners took notice, too. The other clerks and some of the associate lawyers (those not yet partners) became jealous and began referring to me as "Golden Boy."

I had figured a way to financial security. I convinced myself that my ship had come in. I started my third (the last) year of law school with an offer of full-time employment as a lawyer with this firm—the only stipulation being that I pass the Georgia Bar Exam. "Piece of cake," I told myself. I was on the way to becoming a "person of consequence,"—and would be paid handsomely for it. And I thought to myself, "what could be better than all this?"

There was no study guide for the Georgia Bar Exam in Kentucky, where I went to law school. (I hadn't thought about this!) And to add insult to injury, the Georgia Bar Exam was in February of one's third year of law school. This meant I had to take the Georgia Bar Exam before I even graduated from law school—again, all without the typical bar review course offered to students in Georgia law schools.

I didn't let the odds of passing interfere with my determination. "I mean," I said to myself, "how difficult could this exam be?" So, like someone who was either a genius, or just plain misguided, (I fit properly in the latter category), I took the Georgia Bar Exam in February 1987 without having taken the necessary bar review courses.

But, you know what? Miracles do happen. I passed that bar exam, and was eligible to become a lawyer before even graduating from law school! "Wasn't that something?" I thought to myself. If my high school guidance counselor could see me now! I was truly on my way.

I finished law school in May 1987 and was told to report to work by June. And I did just that. As eager as the firm was for me to get started, I was even more eager to get going. It was a match made in Heaven—prestigious Atlanta law firm and eager beaver young lawyer. I couldn't have been more proud or more excited. (As always, I was also scared out of my mind!)

No sooner than I started, however, did I realize I had made a big mistake. For I came to realize that the practice of law wasn't about the seeking of justice, at least not to the level I had imagined. (In all my years of practicing in private firms, I don't think

I once heard anyone discussing "justice.") As I quickly learned, the private practice of law was about two things—winning cases, sometimes at almost any cost, and making money. Frankly, for me, a law firm environment was literally toxic. The practice of law tested my values in ways I found upsetting. Frankly, the practice of law began to eat away at my idealistic soul.

After six years with my first firm, I simply couldn't take the environment any longer. So in the summer of 1993, I went to work for a very small firm located in the suburbs. Upon adding me, we were three lawyers strong!

Initially, I loved it at my new firm. The environment was much more conducive to my needs and values. We all worked hard for our clients, but we also gave consideration to client costs and the possibility of resolving conflict through avenues other than litigation. We even gave consideration to our employee's (and our own) quality of life!

I was proud of our small firm and the reputation we garnered over the years. It was at this firm that I made partner (another milestone I coveted for so long but which turned out to become meaningless to me). But after ten years, my anxiety and depression were taking a serious toll. I struggled mightily to find the strength to even smile. Though I always have given 100% to, and done well for, my clients, it was pretty clear to me that the law business wasn't going to be my calling forever.

By this time, I was in deep with psychiatric treatments. In early 2002, I was hospitalized (for the first of three times) for major depression, and it was in 2003 that I took my most drastic step in my psychiatric care—ECT or "shock therapy" as it is commonly known.

My series of ECT treatments frightened my law partners (not to mention my wife!) It was clear to me they wondered just how ill I really was—and whether I could handle the pressures of being a partner in a law firm—even a small one. The writing was on the wall. My partners didn't want to be partners with me any longer. Given my health challenges, they suggested I might be better suited to step back into an "associate attorney" role. (This would have allowed me to concentrate solely on legal work without the headaches that went with running a business. They knew I loved the challenges of a legal case, and also was effective as a lawyer. So they offered this as a possible solution.) But I was too proud to take a downgraded position. So, I knew I had to go. To their credit, my partners let me figure all this out on my own. No one asked me to leave. I stayed with the firm a while longer before resigning.

I left my firm toward the very end of 2004. At first I didn't know what I was going to do with myself. I wondered whether I was burned out of the practice of law. I thought about taking some time off and finding another career path.

But the more I thought about it, I had to admit I really loved certain parts of the practice of law. I loved helping clients resolve problems or close a business transaction. I enjoyed the intellectual challenges—an effective lawyer must be able to think creatively, and I welcomed this. In my mind at the time, I thought that maybe what I didn't like about the practice of law was having partners and trying to manage other attorneys and the administrative staff. Within days of deciding to leave my firm, I decided I'd give law one last shot. But this time, I was going to do things my way. I was going to start a solo practice. I vowed to open the doors the first business day of January 2005 with a simple name—The Carver Firm.

I opened The Carver Firm with great enthusiasm. I loved my small office space. I took a lot of care decorating it the way I wanted. It was a cool office if I do say so myself. Sure enough, the first business day of January 2005, The Carver Firm was open for business. In just a matter of a few short weeks, I had the office all set up—all the furnishings, equipment, even a secretary to greet new clients. I was set to finally begin a law firm with one thing in mind—seeking justice.

My job was the epitome of total freedom. In addition to a few clients I brought from my old firm, I was getting new clients almost immediately. The first few months were great.

Soon enough, however, I saw the writing on the wall again. Within several months, I knew there was a good chance I was not going to make it. I had let the pendulum swing too far. I took in anyone needing legal help whether they could pay or not (and many at least claimed they could not.) I was under the assumption that if I simply gave justice my all, the money part would take care of itself. This was an enormous miscalculation. I learned quickly that good works could not be my guide as a business endeavor.

I borrowed enough money within the first year that I was starting to get concerned. To alleviate my worries, I starting cashing in my 401(k) funds to provide some breathing room. But I blew through that quickly. Next, I used my good name and credit to borrow substantial sums of money. (I continued to convince myself that things would eventually turn around.)

But before I knew it, I was deep in debt. I had helped a lot of folks solve a lot of problems—but at what cost? Well, to be perfectly frank, at the cost of virtually every material thing I had. All the while, Ann was oblivious to most of this. She was busy with her career and trying to keep some sense of normalcy for our girls in the midst of my breakdown and was not keeping up with how I was managing The Carver Firm. She knew that handling legal cases was relatively easy for me, and she didn't ask about the finances.

As it turned out, I was essentially broke by mid-2007. I had proved to myself that I was a complete failure. I was finally convinced that the practice of law was not a profession, but a business—just like any other business—there was no room for an idealist.

Once again, I turned myself over to the psychiatrists and staff at the hospital. I didn't know exactly what I wanted, but I felt like I had failed at everything I had tried. I remember wanting somehow to be delivered from all my responsibilities. I wanted out of a normal, modern-day life. I wanted just one thing—peace of mind. That's all I really wanted in the entire world—for my mind just to slow down and be at peace. I don't think I've ever felt lower in my life.

What can I say, except psychiatric hospitals are a trip! It's every bit as bad as you might imagine, but, then again, in some ways, a blessing. One thing I did not like. Everyone, from the physicians to the staff to my fellow patients, said I did not look like I belonged. I hated this. I mean, I was hurting inside, too. Just because I did not smell, or wear mismatched clothes, or did not have matted hair, did not mean I was not suffering. I felt betrayed by the psychiatric community. I remember thinking, "what does it take to convince anyone I need help?" (Looking back on it, I think what everyone was trying to say is that I had it together more than most who came in. Yes, I needed help, but I at least had a real chance to get better.)

The worst thing about being in a psychiatric hospital is the initial understanding that you have lost your freedom. You see very quickly that all doors are locked and you have no way out! Your first thought is to find someone who looks reasonable, and say, "okay, look, I'm okay, I promise I won't kill myself and I promise to project the image that I'm completely normal, but will you let me out of here?" But you realize early on that the answer is "no." You realize early on that you have failed in a big way, and you are going to have to pay a steep price for this. Everyone was required to stay long enough to either, a) convince his or her doctor that he or she was no longer a threat to himself or herself or anyone else, or b) that no form of insurance or government assistance was going to continue to pay for treatment. (It's amazing how quickly one was released when no more funds were available to be tapped!)

The psychiatric hospitals taught me a couple valuable lessons. First, it taught me how blessed I really am. I might have been depressed, but this was nothing compared to what I saw. For example, I saw young girls who were so disturbed that they had cut their wrists (whole arms, really) to shreds trying to kill themselves. (I always found the cutters to be the sweetest of patients.) I saw many, many homeless people who checked themselves in just to escape the elements for a short while. I met those who literally had no one—I mean NO ONE—in their lives. These folks were so lonesome they no longer even realized it.

I met many battered wives and girlfriends. I met a lot of addicts. And I met a lot of folks who were just plain nuts. I began to understand why a lot of people felt I didn't belong. Believe me, I was not the typical patient. But I also wasn't the pious type. Every once in a while, a rich, stockbroker-type addict would come in. You could always tell these types from the get-go. They all had great haircuts, wore expensive suits (even if crumpled from their latest high), and thought they were better than everyone else. The majority of the patient population (including me) despised these guys. I mean, give me a break. Here you are—brought in handcuffs to a mental facility—and you are thinking you are better than everyone else because your bank account is full. Without fail, these were the guys who slept in, refused to take part in classes (not even puppy therapy, my favorite) and lost all privileges from the start. It always took these jerks weeks to learn the way out. No one liked, or respected, these guys. They were on their own. For once, their social standing meant nothing.

In a psychiatric hospital, one is treated as a child. Upon entry, you must give up most all possessions, especially anything that you might use to hurt yourself—shoestrings, belts, and razors. You are left with pants you have to continually keep pulling up and shoes with no laces. This is demeaning. But I guess it is also necessary.

The most demeaning thing about a psychiatric hospital is the constant reminder of how you have lost everyone's trust. Everyone who worked there assumed you would attempt to kill yourself with any given opportunity. One time, Ann came to visit and she brought Caroline and Chloe. Given it was Christmas (yes—another reason to feel like crap—in a mental hospital and your children visit you on Christmas), my girls brought me a gift. I remember it was wrapped in beautiful holiday paper. I opened the gift—a beautiful scarf from *Brooks Brothers*. As the girls knew, I absolutely love scarves. But, as it turned out, I couldn't keep it. The guards prohibited it as it was seen as something I could use to hang myself. I had to send it back home with them. That was a low point for sure.

As you can see, in a psychiatric hospital, you are told when to do anything and everything. You are told when to wake up, when to eat, when to exercise, when to focus on the therapy you need to get better, when to relax, and when to got to bed. And if you do not follow the rules, this means a longer stay for you. I learned this quickly, and settled in and tried to adapt as best as I could.

From that last hospital stay, I started to think about the possibility of other career options. I never returned to the traditional practice of law. I still practice, probably always will. But I do it now completely on my own terms—for clients and causes that I believe in wholeheartedly. And I learned that my financial problems were not insurmountable. I finally came clean with Ann as to the true state of my business finances. While my career had plummeted, hers had thrived. (At some point she saw the writing on the wall and decided she needed to be financially independent.) Together, we made a financial plan, and she helped me start digging my way out of debt. I agreed to work from home and tend to the girls' needs at home. (This turned out to be a true blessing, as I began to reconnect with them. Over the years, I had simply lost touch with them.)

With the few cases I have now, It's about addressing wrongs. In an odd sort of way, I have reached a point that the practice of law means something special to me. When I gave up any notion of it being a business for me, it finally became what I wanted it to become—a public service of seeking justice.

Truth is, I don't have what it takes to be a successful lawyer by the current standards of making vast sums of money. For one, I don't care about money—never have. Moreover, I despise the self-importance so many lawyers attach to themselves. In my opinion, there is no higher calling than being a true lawyer—a champion of justice. But, sadly, there are very few of these lawyers left anymore. No, we now only have those who are in the "practice of law." There's a world of difference between a person who seeks justice and one who "practices law." That's solely my opinion—but I think I'm right. It would be another two years after that last hospital stay before I would find and start to pursue my next "calling,"—writing.

Despite suffering for as long as I can remember, I did not seek psychiatric treatment until early middle age—sometime in 2001—in my very late 30's. (I'm now almost 50.) What I lost in time, I made up for in my aggressive pursuit of healing. I have undertaken just about every type of psychiatric treatment offered. Many helped—at least for a while. Some did not help at all. But medical care has been indispensable for me. To this day, I rely on a limited regimen of psychiatric medication to help alleviate my most severe anxiety.

I tried everything with enthusiasm and hope. I began with talk therapy (hoping a re-hashing of my life would bring some clarity), quickly moved to behavioral therapy (striving to change unproductive behavioral habits), and then started the tangled web of psychiatric medication.

Medication became a nightmare fast. Indeed, over the course of two years, I tried, in various dosages and combinations, a vast array of old and new drugs. I have at one time or another taken Lithium, Zoloft, Prozac, Ambien, Zyprexa, Risperdal, Seroquel, Thorazine, Anafranil, Desyrel, Effexor, Lexapro, Luvox, Nardil, Paxil, Remeron, Tofranil, Wellbutrin, Depakote, Lamictal, Topamax, Ativan, BuSpar, Klonopin, Xanax, Cymbalta, and Abilify. That pretty much covers it! During one period, I was taking 23 pills per day. I was a walking pharmacy—and at times a walking zombie—my meds at times numbed me to the point of merely breathing.

In 2003, things took an even more serious turn. I was placed in a psychiatric facility and was advised to undergo ECT (electro-convulsive therapy). Saved for the most treatment-resistant depressives, this was supposedly my last good shot at beating depression. My wife and I were frightened about the procedure. (Ann flat out did not want me to do it.) Despite the strides made in the treatment, when the topic of ECT is broached, most folks still think of the films, *One Flew Over The Cuckoo's Nest* or *A Beautiful Mind*. Frankly, most folks think of it as a bizarre and harrowing notion. And, frankly, that's not far from the truth.

To this day, no one understands how ECT actually works. In a nutshell, ECT is a treatment whereby brain seizures are electrically induced in an anesthetized patient. In general, the treatment is effective for a period of months, and sometimes longer. Many times, patients receive multiple series of treatments over their lives.

Other than my wife and daughters, not one person ever visited me during my treatments. During it all, I received exactly one card and one bouquet of flowers. The stigma of ECT was just too much for others to publicly (or even privately) stand by me. And frankly, I was disappointed with the outcome. After my prescribed series, I felt relief for only a few months. And despite this small window of respite, it cost me some measure of my short-term memory and some memory loss lingers to this day.

Within a short period of time, I lost all confidence that the psychiatric field had anything of substance (pardon the pun) to offer me. I should have continued the search for alternative treatments. But I lost confidence in the psychiatric community. I felt like a burned-out lab rat. I lost all confidence I would ever really get better at all. I was beginning to descend into the most dangerous of realms—resignation.

"We've got to find that kid again."

It was only my second meeting with a new psychiatrist, Warren Jacobs, M.D. He made this statement with his customary smile and pleasant tone as he handed me back the photograph he had asked me to bring in. During our first session, he asked me to bring in a photograph of myself as a child. He said I could bring anything as long as it was one of a happy memory. I found an old photograph taken of me when I was about six years old. Smiling with no front teeth, I was proudly hoisting a small carp I had caught from my grandfather's farm pond.

Truth is, I thought the idea of bringing in the photograph was sort of silly. I knew where this was headed. We were going to start at the very beginning and move forward. I had by then long lost count of the number of psychiatrists and therapists I had seen for treatment. I would guess Dr. Jacobs was probably about number twelve.

I had previously given up on all forms of medical help. But I had no choice but to continue nonetheless. In the fall of 2007, my wife and I were trying to save our marriage, and the couples' therapist we were seeing would not continue unless I agreed to resume psychiatric treatment. Ann was adamant that I follow our therapist's advice and I wanted to save our marriage. So, per instructions from our marriage counselor, it was back to the couch for me. I was once again in formal psychiatric treatment with my new psychiatrist.

Turns out, I loved Dr. Jacobs. I loved him from the start. Unlike the patient mills I had been to previously, Dr. Jacobs' office was warm and inviting. The lobby had trendy and up-to-date magazines and played soothing music for the waiting patients. The waiting area was never crowded and Dr. Jacobs was always punctual. I never waited more than five minutes to get to see him. (All this may seem trivial, but I had been to plenty of offices where I was always met by an impersonal receptionist behind frosted glass that was never opened unless absolutely necessary. Interaction was kept to a minimum. The receptionist was there seemingly only to ensure compliance with the PAYMENT MUST BE RENDERED AT TIME OF SERVICE sign. After the transaction, the door was slid to its closed position. We patients were then forced to sit and endure the uncomfortable and agonizing wait to hear our names called. I don't know how many *Reader's Digest, Highlights* (yes, the children's magazine), and psychiatric pamphlets I have read in those lobbies, but it would easily number in the hundreds.

But Dr. Jacobs was different. I decided early on he was my kind of guy. His office was adorned with Native American images and folk art. He even had an acoustic guitar in the corner. He was getting on in age, probably late 60's. But he wore his hair straight back and in a little ponytail. He dressed casually and always with some sort of funky shirt. He seemed a bit Bohemian to me and I was drawn to him. He actually looked at me and smiled the first time we met. He was like no psychiatrist I had ever been around. He was a man who was the very definition of compassion.

Dr. Jacobs single-handedly restored my faith in the field of psychiatry. Sadly, after only working together a short time, he suffered a recurrence of cancer and died. He wrote me a very sweet note just before he lost his battle. He said he wished he could say goodbye in person. I really loved that man.

The last "machine" at which I've directed my rage is myself. And I saved "myself" for my harshest of rage. As I have been reminded many times by many people, it truly is pointless to harbor ill will toward institutions or organizations over which one has very little or no control. (I know this to be true, but I'm still in the process of learning this completely.) But I know I can change myself.

I was born broke and remain broke to this day. I'm not talking about broke in the financial sense. I mean I was born with a broken brain—I have never been able to process emotions very well and with the appropriate degree of normal human reason. For most of my life, I've felt either scared out of my mind (remember, the Horrible Thing) or numb to the point I could feel nothing.

My broken brain also led to a broken heart. I finally realized that almost everything and everyone was far from perfect. Even more so, that everything and everyone was so riddled with faults that it's sometimes difficult to see their goodness and beauty. This may seem to most an inherent truth, but for me, it was a disappointing revelation that was difficult to get my head around. And second, I came to see (right before my unbelieving eyes) that I was also far, far from perfect. I failed in ways I would have never imagined possible for me. It's like I was watching some stranger from afar. But, I finally had to admit, that, yes, it was none other than yours truly going in the wrong direction at every turn. I failed more miserably and fell farther than any of the institutions that disappointed anyone or me I knew personally. I was crushed and deeply ashamed. It took me years to finally realize (several years ago now) that neither I nor anyone else could possibly live up to the standard of perfection I had set for us all.

When I finally accepted that everybody is human after all (including myself)—with all sorts of flaws, shortcomings, hidden agendas, and failures, I simply quit trying. I stopped trying to be loving, caring, kind, or compassionate. I stopped caring about much of anything at all. My existence (for the years of about mid-2006 to mid-2009) was one of complete misery.

Perhaps the worst of my faults at this point was my total self-absorption and self-centeredness. I had simply lost the ability to see anything or anyone beyond myself. During this time period, I simply wanted to die. (Indeed, a couple times I saved up much of my anti-anxiety medication—several months' worth—and took them along with enormous amounts of alcohol. I hoped to go to sleep and never wake up. I was simply done. I wanted the screen to go completely black. I remember praying to God that, at least for me, there would be no such thing as an afterlife. I couldn't stomach the notion of existing any longer—even if it were in a paradise called Heaven.

But both times I awoke the next morning.

HEARTS SMOTHERED IN GREED

It is with a sad heart that I write today's post. I try my best to stay positive with this blog, but every now and again, something will hit me hard and I must speak my mind. Today is one of those days.

I just read the news that Transocean Ltd., the owner of the oil rig that exploded in the Gulf of Mexico last year injuring 17 workers and killing 11 others (along with doing untold damage to wildlife and the environment), claimed it had its "best year" in safety. Further, Transocean, Ltd. reported a $200,000 salary increase for its President and CEO (increasing salary from $900,000 to $1.1 mil.) on top of his bonus of $374,062.

Now, in fairness, after the news outlets reported this story, Transocean Ltd. issued an additional statement acknowledging its boastful statement "may have been insensitive." Huh? May have been insensitive? Are you kidding me? I ask you—how could this company, in good conscience, award its President/CEO a salary increase and bonus totaling more than a half million dollars? And why am I writing about this in a blog about discovering and becoming oneself?

The answers are simple. Let's look at another example of a recent "bonus" to a successful executive. In 2009, President Barack Obama was awarded the Nobel Peace Prize and received approximately $1.4 million. What did the President do with this windfall? He donated every dime to charity—split it among ten organizations, including the United Negro College Fund and five other groups that help kids pay for college, donated to the Fisher House, which provides housing for families with loved ones at VA hospitals, and donated to the Clinton-Bush Haiti Fund to rebuild the earthquake-ravaged nation.

I suggest to you that these two gentlemen are a contrast in what it means to have a heart. Sadly, too many times in our society, our hearts are smothered in greed. I challenge Transocean Ltd.'s President/CEO to donate his salary increase and bonus to the victims of the Gulf of Mexico disaster. I hope he will accept this challenge. Time will tell. "But Reg," you say, "it just doesn't work like that. Transocean Ltd. has other funds set aside to deal with this tragedy. You're naïve." Maybe so. One thing is for certain—I'm no businessman. I am the last person anyone would want in charge of a corporation. I don't have the drive necessary to, well, "ensure optimal value for shareholders" or "build shareowner wealth" or whatever the corporate speak of the day is.

But I do know that leadership with a heart can be good for business, too. I look at companies like Google, TOMS, Zappos and Whole Food Market and I know one can run a successful business and also have a heart. I know company employees and their families can be truly valued and much can be done to ensure a company employee and his or her family is taken care of—especially in time of need or tragedy.

My friends, we as a people must do a better job of opening our hearts. And I'm including myself here. I'm far from exempt in not always having an open heart. At times my heart has been smothered in a whole host of destructive emotions. But we have to try. We have to do better. The world can ill afford for the few rich to continue to hold onto the wealth they have. We have to open our hearts and pocketbooks to those in need. And especially in instances where to do so will in no way affect our own ability to afford all we could ever really need or want.

I don't mean to single out Transocean Ltd. and its President/ CEO. Corporate greed is everywhere and rampant. But this unfortunate story just strikes me as a prime example of the height of hypocrisy. Transocean Ltd. pays lip service to its grief over the loss of lives, but then it turns right around and pads the pockets of those in charge of a company who played at least some part in the largest oil spill in history. This is absurd.

Let's use my juxtaposition of Transocean Ltd. executives and the President as a lesson for us all. Let's uncover our hearts—our true hearts—the type of heart exhibited by our President. Let's reach out when we can. If we could just do that, the world would no longer know starvation, problems of homelessness, and poor education. Folks could be treated with a measure of dignity. We all deserve that, and especially from those at the "top echelon" of society.

Please, let us vow to show our true heart—the heart that is inside all of us. It may be smothered at present. Greed's sticky tentacles may have gotten hold of us. If so, let's vow to untangle ourselves. Let's give when and with what we can. Let's strive to be good and generous to one another. That's not too much to ask. Yes, I may be naïve, but I do know that.

PS: So, I'm watching CNN late at night before this post is set to go up (at midnight) and on AC360 it has just been announced that Transocean Ltd. executives have decided to donate their bonuses to a relief fund for victims of the Gulf of Mexico oil spill, saying it's just the right thing to do! This is indeed the right thing to do and wonderful news! These executives are opening their hearts and wallets to co-workers and their families in need.

Wow. I feel better about our world and my fellow human beings. But honestly, I'm not shocked. Nothing shocks me anymore. And this is especially true about the possibility of good things happening. I have faith they will. And they do. Again, thank you to the Transocean Ltd. executives. Your willingness to do this speaks volumes about you and about the best part of being human. We can almost always right a wrong. We just have to be courageous enough to open our hearts.

Sources for this post include the CNN article entitled "Gulf oil rig owner apologizes for calling 2010 'best year' ever" by The CNN Wire Staff, April 4, 2011.

A MATTER OF PRIDE

I've been pretty low this past weekend. It happens—the past will start to haunt and work on me. Perhaps the lowest point was over a dinner we were having with new acquaintances—the parents of a dear friend of my daughter, Chloe. These are lovely folks—open-minded and very interesting. These guys haven't lived in Georgia all that long and the subject of making friends came up.

The father noted that he considered his greatest wealth to be his friends. He asked me if I understood what he was saying and if I felt the same way. I assured him I understood exactly what he was saying, but I said I had to admit I didn't feel the same way as I could not, at that moment, think of a single friend I have excepting my wife (who, I'm so thankful, is a dear friend.) It felt good to answer the question honestly and not to try to come up with some bullshit for an answer. But, indeed, to have to admit that particular truth did hurt my pride.

Coincidentally, I have been re-reading a book I have had for a long time. The Low Road To New Heights, by Wellington Boone, is essentially a call to what the author considers the only path to meaningful success. That path is total humility. Indeed, it calls on each of us to be more Christ-like and give up the hardest trait of all for humans to relinquish—pride. Notes Boone, "From a great messianic psalm (Psalm 22:7) which Jesus quoted on the cross, comes this confession from His inmost being: 'But I am a worm, and no man; a reproach of men, and despised by the people.' . . . Jesus called himself a worm because He led a surrendered life, and died a surrendered death. When it was time to return to His Father, He could say, 'It is finished.' (John

19:30) He had never changed His mind about His surrender. He was the greatest example of humility the world has ever seen, and we are called to follow Him in His humility."*

Perhaps also coincidentally (perhaps not as I think about all this), over the weekend I also watched the movie Gandhi. Indeed, Mahatma Gandhi was also a great example of humility and a man who also let go of pride. As pointed out in his wonderful book, Gandhi's Passion: The Life and Legacy of Mahatma Gandhi, Stanley Wolpert notes that, "after acquiring more political power than any other Indian of the previous century of British rule had enjoyed, he rejected all the power perquisites coveted by others the world over. He refused to travel any way but by foot or in third-class railway carriages and retreated to the Spartan simplicity of remote village ashrams he founded whenever he was jailed in a British prison. Gandhi's seemingly eccentric or at any rate curiously contradictory behavior, his rejection of all 'normal' pleasures, acquisitive and sensual, and his oft-repeated retreat from the brink of victory can best be understood in light of his passionate resolve to suffer the experience in daily life all the pain and deepest sorrow sustained by India's poorest peasants and outcasts. He shivered naked in winter as they did and bore the scalding heat of central India's summers without complaint. When the Congress offered him complete control over its national machinery and the crown of its presidency, he invariably declined, grooming younger men to wear what he called the 'crown of thorns.' He abandoned the organization he had revitalized when it became too high and mighty, too rich and greedy, for his passionate nature."**

When I awoke this morning, it all began to make sense to me. This weekend was a test. I had passed in being honest with my dinner guest. But I had failed in allowing it to hurt my pride. To find wholeness, indeed to heal, I must learn to, and, in fact, give up the trait I've been so guilty of carrying through it all—pride. I said a prayer this morning and asked God to relieve me of my pride. It goes without saying that I will never reach this to the extent of Jesus or Gandhi, but I believe that the striving for such relinquishment will stand me in good stead for the continued road ahead.

Only moments after I said my prayers, I received a text from an old law school buddy of mine. He said he's been going through my blog posts—one by one in the order they were published. The one he said touched him the most was Cooling The Flames (January 12, 2011) about compassionate and non-judgmental listening. He said he wanted to work on that. Rather than puff up with pride inside, I just smiled and felt thankful it had touched him. Importantly, I also remembered that he was someone I could still call a friend. I had been mistaken with my statement over the weekend. I'm extremely grateful for his friendship.

Indeed, striving to give up pride will be formidable challenge, but one I'm excited to undertake. Maybe the "low road" will in fact lead to success—not the type of success that mankind exalts these days, but true success—just the kind of success I am in need of.

---

* The Low Road To New Heights, by Wellington Boone.
** Gandhi's Passion: The Life and Legacy of Mahatma Gandhi, by Stanley Wolpert.

THE SELF-SABOTEUR

"All men are by nature equal, made all of the same Earth by one Workman; and however we deceive ourselves, as dear unto God is the poor peasant as the mighty prince."

Plato

"Whatever you want in life, other people are going to want it, too. Believe in yourself enough to accept the idea that you have an equal right to it."

Diane Sawyer

We live in an imperfect, sometimes downright unfair, world. It seems at times that, no matter how hard we try, there are others out there trying to sabotage our happiness or progress. I think we all have experienced this from time to time.

But, as much as others try to sabotage us, there are certain of us who face an even more menacing enemy—ourselves. I've been told many times by therapists and others that I fall into this category. Please ask yourself if you could be in the same boat, and, if so, please take steps to address this issue.

I believe the self-saboteur is a person who, for any host of reasons, develops low self-esteem or self-worth. (Obviously low self-esteem or self-worth can stem from many causes—poverty, abuse, guilt over past transgressions, and many others.) Armed with a negative view of himself or herself, the self-saboteur is convinced he or she does not deserve what others deserve—sometimes this includes even basic needs like proper nutrition or decent clothing.

(At one very low point in my life, I lost 60 pounds quickly without even trying. I just basically stopped eating. My psychiatrist told me I suffered from such low self-esteem that I wasn't even allowing myself decent food. He was right; and, to this day, while I've gained some weight back, I still only eat one meal a day, even when I hunger for more.)

We self-saboteurs know, deep down, that this is abnormal, for we know, on an intellectual level, that we have the same basic needs and wants as everyone else. We also push ourselves to succeed much like others. The difference comes into play, however, just at the time we are on the cusp of obtaining a want, need or success at something. The self-saboteur, feeling inferior to his fellow man, when getting close to obtaining a material possession or reaching a goal, will start to feel guilty about the joy such will bring. This "guilt phase" tends to last for a while (how long depends on the individual), and will eventually pass. But the whole absurd pattern repeats itself again and again.

If I am resonating with you (and you know who you are), you must start finding a way to believe in your heart what you already know in your head—no matter our skin color, sexual orientation, financial status, age, state of health, our philosophical or religious convictions or absolutely anything else, we are equal in that we all are human beings. We all deserve basic necessities. Moreover, there is nothing wrong with having a few luxuries if we can afford them.

Life is meant to bring joy and happiness. Everyone deserves at least the opportunity to seek this and attain it if possible. Please do what you need to do to really teach yourself you are everyone's equal. It may only take a simple reminder from time to time. It may also take seeking professional help. Whatever it is, do what it takes to learn this truth.

Life is going to bring some pain—no doubt. We should also seek some joy along the way of dealing with our difficulties. Otherwise, we are simply stuck in a constant state of conflict. This robs us of joy and happiness. Bottom line—we all deserve happiness. It's that simple. You can get about the business of learning and believing this, or you can wallow in misery. It's really up to you.

GUARDING OUR ORBIT

"What we see we become. Choose your seeing wisely."

Deepak Chopra

I absolutely love books. And I've learned that nearly all newly published books are released on Tuesdays. You can be assured, therefore, that at some point every Tuesday, I will be checking out Barnes & Noble, The New York Times Book Review, and other websites to find out what new books I may be interested in reading.

Yesterday, I read the above Chopra quote just before checking online for new books. As I perused the new releases (usually limited to biographies and memoirs), I thought about this quote. I noticed that what I search for now is entirely different from what I used to search for. In the worst of my times, I was drawn to books about depression, suicide, and, in general, lives in turmoil. I was noticing yesterday, however, that these days I skip over these works and look for more uplifting offerings.

Deepak Chopra is exactly right. What we see we do become. By constantly focusing on the negative, on lives in crisis, I was becoming more and more negative. At times, my world became one big orbit of negativity. And it wasn't limited to what I saw. As I think about it, I chose negativity in almost all my other senses, too. I was drawn to negative or depressing movies and television programs. I was not eating regularly, and not choosing the right foods when I did eat. Many folks I associated with had a negative impact on me.

Somehow, slowly over time, I began to switch to a more positive orbit and one that is more reflective of my true self. This has made an immeasurable difference in the way I see the world and in my emotional stability. These days I strive to surround myself with truth and with positivity. I strive to stay more connected with my family and to make wise choices regarding friends. I guard my orbit fiercely. Frankly, it's my only real chance to be my best self.

We must all decide what we will allow our minds to experience. We adults especially have a good bit of control over what we choose to focus on and what we choose to ignore or at least not become mired in. I would ask each one of you (as I constantly ask myself these days) to continuously examine whether you are guarding your orbit in a responsible and positive way. If you are not, I suggest you reflect on ways you may be able to do this. You just might find (as I did) that changing orbits may change your life and outlook in a remarkably positive way.

THE FUTILITY OF BLAME

"All blame is a waste of time. No matter how much fault you find with another, and regardless of how much you blame him, it will not change you . . . . You may succeed in making another feel guilty about something by blaming him, but you won't succeed in changing whatever it is about you that is making you unhappy."
Wayne Dyer

"The best day of your life is the one which you decide your life is your own. No apologies or excuses. No one to . . . blame. The gift is yours—it is an amazing journey—and you alone are responsible for the quality of it. This is the day your life really begins."
Bob Mowad

I've just started my twenty-fifth year practicing law. I still remember like it was yesterday how excited I was in high school when I decided I wanted to become a lawyer. I had dreams of righting wrongs, helping folks to resolve hopeless disputes, of seeking justice. I spent a lot of time studying law and the legal system. I have given many days and nights pursuing victories on behalf of clients.

In my career, I have had the blessing of seeing justice. But, to be honest, these sightings have been few and far between. Mostly, I've seen folks simply hiring professional help in fruitless quests for placing blame and exacting revenge. Even with cases of genuine merit, rarely have I seen anyone truly satisfied with the outcome of a lawsuit.

The older I get, the more disillusioned I have become with the practice of law. Indeed, I am now mostly pursuing a writing career. I believe this is the case because I have come to believe, no I know, that almost all litigation is unnecessary and an utter waste of time and resources—monetary and human.

Why would I argue that most legal cases are a waste of time? The answer is really quite simple. I believe the vast majority of legal cases do not involve the seeking of justice, but the placement of blame and exacting of punishment. And in the end, a formal rendering of a verdict proves ultimately to be of no satisfaction—there is usually no meaningful apologies or offers of amends, and, alternatively, no real forgiveness—there is only a formal placement of blame, an ultimately hollow victory for one side.

The seeking and placement of blame is an absolutely futile endeavor. This is the truth for several reasons. First, it involves energy expended in the past. (It's always a far better idea to live in the present and prepare for the future.) Secondly, it involves an enormous consumption of time and energy—and only to almost always receive nothing or very little in return. Finally, it brings forth negative emotions—anger and resentment—and fosters conflict rather than resolution. As Dr. Dyer says above, the placement of blame only accomplishes a negative—making someone feel guilty—but ultimately produces no or very little in terms of a positive result.

Please choose wisdom over a futile expending of time and energy. Sure, there may be times where someone may pull one over on you. But, even so, on balance you will usually come out ahead. By refusing to seek or place blame, you retain all your precious energy and time for positive or worthwhile endeavors.

Take the seeking and placement of blame out of your orbit. Don't even give it the time of day. The few times you will be hurt by this stance will be far outweighed by the times you will be rewarded in countless positive ways. I feel strongly I am seeing this as a truth you can trust.

REVENGE

"Revenge is always the weak pleasure of a little and
narrow mind."

Juvenal

"You have heard that it was said, 'An eye for an eye
and a tooth for a tooth.' But I say to you, offer no
resistance to one who is evil. When someone strikes
you on your right cheek, turn the other one
to him as well."

Jesus of Nazareth—Bible,
Matthew 5:38-39 (NAV)

As we all know, on Sunday, May 1, the United States
conducted an operation and ended the life of Osama bin Laden.
Like a lot of folks around the world, I thought the US did what it
had to do. I believe the US owed it to its own citizens and others
to stop a terrorist from what would assuredly be more attacks and
deaths of innocent people around the world.

But I was saddened to see the celebrations over the death.
It seemed to me that a lot of folks viewed bin Laden's death as
revenge for his past acts. All the reactions started me to thinking
about the concept of revenge and the emotional toll it yields on
the one seeking and, in fact, exacting revenge.

Dictionary.com defines revenge as, "exacting punishment or
expiation for a wrong on behalf of, especially in a resentful or
vindictive spirit." I've grown to despise the concept of "revenge." I
have been a practicing lawyer for 24 years and a practicing human

being for 48 years. In my days, I have witnessed a lot of revenge. And, sadly, I have seen it utterly destroy the person exacting it.

Revenge for revenge's sake is not only worthless, in my opinion it actually takes a far greater toll on the one exacting the revenge. In the extreme or when practiced often, revenge will destroy one's emotional well-being. To me, it is one of the most powerful acts one can do to hurt oneself. It may feel pleasurable for an instant, but, with the passage of time, revenge will start to eat at the avenger to a far greater extent than to the one against whom revenge is taken.

This is the case because I believe human beings are hard-wired to love and revere peace far more than conflict. In exacting revenge, we are creating conflict for ourselves. This conflict will eat at one's soul long after the momentary pleasure of the act of revenge. I know this through personal experience, and I have witnessed it many times with others.

Please take this advice to heart. The next time someone has wronged you or a friend or loved one, try forgiveness. Try turning the other cheek. It may be difficult to do, I know. But I guarantee you that if you do, you will eventually find peace in your heart for your wisdom. You will be rewarded with peace and a feeling of tranquility. And this is a far better feeling, and indeed far healthier, than exacting revenge. Try to trust me on this.

These are lessons I have learned the hard way. But, I can attest to the truth of them unequivocally. You will come much closer to your best self if you will exercise restraint and forgiveness in all your dealings with others. You will gain far more peace from this response than from revenge any day. Moreover, you might just teach the wrongdoer a lesson in the process. Your act of forgiveness and "turning the other cheek" might actually work to deter a wrongdoer the next time. This would be benefit to all.

Please be careful when dealing with the concept of revenge. Leave revenge to its own process. This is the best we can offer in our daily lives. Always strive to offer the best response you can in any situation. In doing so, you will find that love and forgiveness will reap far greater rewards in the long run. You will know in your heart that you have given your best at the most trying of times.

In order to be your best self, you must always strive for wisdom. Exacting revenge is the farthest thing form wisdom I know. You must trust me on this. I know what I'm talking about.

MANNEQUIN DEPRESSION

"Always remember that you are absolutely unique.
Just like everyone else."
                                        Margaret Mead

In the last couple months, I've noticed that my meds need tweaking. I'm feeling lethargic during the day and am having trouble sleeping at night. I will be seeing my psychiatrist soon and we can address this. She is very in tune with my psyche and always has ideas for adjustment. She is always open to suggestions from me as well.

I love this about my psychiatrist. Over the course of my treatment, I probably have seen about a dozen therapists and psychiatrists. Of this number, I would say that probably four of them really tried to see me as a unique person with unique needs. Now, this is not meant to suggest that all psychiatrists are this way. I can only base my opinions on my own personal experience. But I've learned over the years that, to get the best treatment, you must find a therapist or psychiatrist who knows the truth that everyone is indeed unique and willing to put in the time and effort to get to know you in a deeply personal way.

The quote at the post's beginning has a kind of humorous bent to it. But Margaret Mead was a renowned cultural anthropologist and she meant this in a serious way. Each one of us is unique and, yes, this applies to everyone. This is especially true of the combination of brain make-up and personality. Psychiatrists, more than anyone, should know this truth.

What I'm trying to say today is that psychiatric treatment is like no other. Take the example of an orthodontist. With a child's crooked teeth, it's easy to apply some braces (the same braces he places on most all his other patients). With respect to someone with a blockage in coronary arteries, there are basic procedures that apply to most everyone. In my opinion, physicians treating patients for these issues can see us all as mannequins—only the hair and eye color is different. Generally speaking, what works for one works for all.

It's just not this case with psychiatric problems. My friend, if your therapist or psychiatrist sees himself or herself as treating what I call "mannequin depression," you have the wrong caregiver. And it is up to you to figure out whether your psychiatrist is among those in this category. They are out there, and, in my opinion, being treated by one with this mentality is a complete waste of your time. With this type treatment, you will not get better. You don't have even a shred of a chance.

Please do yourself a favor. Take a long, hard look at your therapist or psychiatrist. If you feel he or she is not taking the time to get to really know you and your needs, then let him or her go and find someone who will. You must also educate yourself regarding drug and other treatment options. Most physicians, for reasons not entirely clear to me, will want to prescribe only the latest available medications. Granted, many times these are just what you may need. But many times, an older medication will be more effective for you. (Please don't misunderstand me here. As a patient, you indeed must realize that you are the patient and not the physician. Sometimes there will be very good reasons for not attempting something you suggest. But the physician should at least take the time to explore in good faith any option you suggest.) If you are getting a blank stare while you are discussing your ideas, please, go elsewhere.

I have learned this lesson the hard way—over ten years of working with psychiatrists. Again, while this is simply my opinion, I feel strongly that I know what I'm talking about here. When it comes to your psyche, you are truly unique with truly unique needs. You can trust me on this one.

ANOTHER KIND OF BEGINNING

"Supposing you have tried and failed again and again.
You may have a fresh start any moment you choose,
for this thing we call "failure" is not the falling down,
but the staying down."

Mary Pickford

It bends logic to its breaking point that I ever had the chance to write this book. My two most serious suicide attempts should have proved fatal. Also, because I had fallen so low, my only real chance of getting better was through the love and support of my wife. But as Ann is the one I betrayed the most (I literally put her through Hell at times), it remains a mystery to me why she stuck by me. The level of love and compassion she has shown me has been humbling to say the least. Frankly, it was nothing short of a miracle I had another chance at finding myself and finding peace.

By the summer of 2009, I knew I was at ground zero. Literally. Pretty much everything that had been important in my life thus far was no longer there for me—my career, a spiritual life, and psychiatric care. As I saw it, all these institutions had nothing to offer me any longer. And I didn't even know myself at all anymore. For so long I had pretended to be someone (anyone) other than myself.

Basically, I knew I had to start over—I had to become the real me. But I had no clue whom that person was anymore. I pretended for so long to be something I was not that my true identity all but escaped me.

I vowed to try. And I vowed to do whatever it took to discover myself, and then to be the best whomever I found myself to be. I also vowed that I would strive to be good human being—according to my own definition. For months, this is all I really knew.

My first changes involved my outward appearance—and they were stark and, at first, somewhat unsettling to me. For all my adult life, I looked as though I could be an advertisement for a *Brooks Brothers* catalogue. With my conservative haircut, starched cotton shirts, rep ties, and wingtips, I was the epitome of "buttoned down." And I grew to hate it. The problem was—this is how everyone around me dressed and was also what was expected of me.

I started making changes, and I went all out. I began a years-long process of having my body tattooed. I love tattoos. I viewed my body as one big canvas and I wanted to color it with my story. (One of my psychiatrists frowned on them and said tattoos were a form of self-mutilation. I promptly fired him.)

I also began to dress differently. I traded in all those "hey, I'm a banker" duds for t-shirts, shorts and TOMS. And unless there is something out of the ordinary going on, you will find me in this new uniform every single day.

All this change felt so good to me. Granted, sometimes (well, many times) I would wear long sleeves to hide my new look if I knew I would be seeing people who knew me. But, gradually, over time, and due to the encouragement of Ann, I just let me be me. (There are so many ways in which Ann showed me how to accept and be myself that words fail me. Bottom line, she stayed, and she encouraged me to accept myself and all the blessings I had been given. She wanted more than anything for me to see that it was okay for me to accept the blessings I had been given.)

The next thing I worked on was allowing myself to speak my mind. For so long—years and years—I hid my real views on subjects such as politics and religion. To say that north Fulton County, Georgia is comprised of a majority of traditionally conservative (with respect to religion and politics) folks is like saying Louisville, Kentucky is home to a pretty good annual horse race. I learned to keep my mouth shut when it came to religious and political views.

But I just decided, what the hell—I'm going to be myself—let the chips fall where they may. I said to myself, "folks who know me now pretty much know how I feel." Folks knew I was open-minded in every sense of the word. And most were cool with this. (Deep down, maybe they wouldn't admit it, but I think most people who know me respect me for this over anything else. And with respect to those who don't, they just disappeared from my life. I think it's worked out well for both parties.)

Slowly but surely, I started to become more comfortable in my own colorful skin. The thing is, if you do not pay attention to what anyone else thinks, you can't help but be comfortable! I just vowed to be myself. In my case, it really was that simple.

One exception to openness was a change I made and kept hidden—even from Ann. Beginning in 2005, I began to take courses in Buddhism. I took them in secret because I thought everyone, even Ann, would not accept this. (This is how insecure I remained about being myself. Eventually (and in secret), I took the Refuge Vow, formally committing to following the Buddha. It was some time before I revealed this to Ann. She was initially upset I didn't reveal this from the beginning, but ultimately she came to accept, even embrace my newfound faith. This all reminded me once again that if I could learn to have the self-confidence to be myself, I would find that almost everyone else would accept me as I am.)

Okay, so now I looked and said as I pleased. But for reasons I cannot explain to this day, over the course of the summer of 2009, I made the decision that I was going to make a real effort toward being a better person. I decided I could be a good person and myself all at the same time. (I was really getting confident here!)

Again, I don't know exactly why the decision stuck. I think, more than anything, I simply couldn't live with myself as I was any longer. Frankly, I knew I had to continue to occupy my mind and body for the long haul. I think I simply decided I wanted to learn to do so in peace rather than with the constant conflict to which I had become accustomed. Bottom line, I was no longer willing to accept my life on any terms other those under which I could feel good.

From the summer of 2009, I mostly just thought about change. I took no action toward change, but I did do some serious thinking.

(One exception to doing nothing, we let go of our nanny and I began to re-connect with, and take care of, our daughters. And I took time to take care of our home and most domestic chores—like cooking, the laundry, and minor cleaning. I was beginning to rebuild relationships I had neglected and was beginning to actually be helpful to the family. Ann also agreed to help me dig out of my financial hole, and, thankfully, my debts are now either all paid in full or well on the way to being so.)

But my real progress toward change began to take shape during our family's annual summer vacation to Rosemary Beach, Florida in the summer of 2010. Over the course of that vacation, Ann and I had some long talks about what I and we were going to do in the future. (We both knew it was time to embark on a new journey.) We started to think about what I could do with my interests and talents.

We both knew that I had a lot bottled inside me. I needed to process everything and maybe that would set me on the right course. I was reminded of Dr. Jacobs' suggestion that I start journaling. Sometimes, one can better understand his feelings by committing them to writing.

Together, Ann and I came up with the idea of my starting a blog. The thought of a new career in writing was appealing to me. What better way to test the waters than through a blog?

On August 28, 2010, I had *FindMyOwnCurrent.com* up and running. I published three posts per week on topics relating to becoming one's true self, the arts, Buddhism, and a healthy dose of anything else I wanted to write about. (One post is devoted to making my daughter Chloe's wonderful creamed corn!)

I found I LOVED writing. I focused all my energy on something I felt worthwhile rather than simply continuing to wallow in misery. Through the course of writing my weekly posts, I began to process a lot that had happened in my life. And I began to experience peace I had never known.

I found blogging so much fun I even started a second one—*fromi2us.com*. As much as *FindMyOwnCurrent* focused on finding and being oneself, *fromi2us* explores what could happen if we put others or "the whole" first in our lives.

I wrote and I wrote. I found that my blogs were catching on a bit, and I was slowly building traffic. I heard from folks all over the world who said my posts had helped them or a loved one. I can't describe how good this made me feel. For the first time in my life, I was living a life with a purpose—a purpose I believed in.

I wrote almost 300 blog posts in eighteen months. By the winter of 2012, I felt I had said most of what I wanted to say about being oneself. I stopped writing these posts and said goodbye for the time being. Who knows what the future of them will be? (They remain up to this day, and I'm keeping them up for a while.)

By the end of 2011, I had the idea for this book. I wanted to join my backstory with some of the blog posts I had written. I wanted to tell my story of anxiety, depression, of losing but ultimately finding my way. I wanted to do this for two reasons: 1) I wanted a clear demarcation of the time I had finally reached a point of positive and meaningful change. (The publication of this book is very symbolic of this.); and 2) I wanted to share my story with others in hopes I could make connections and help those who might find encouragement from my story. Depression and other mental ailments are rampant the world over. But many hide their struggles due to the stigma associated with any form of mental illness.

THE WRATH OF GRAPES

"There is no revenge so complete as forgiveness."
Josh Billings

This past Monday morning, I had the pleasure of spending a little time with my good friend from Jamaica. I love spending time with him—he's always upbeat and superb company as he's always both "interested and interesting." No matter how short of a visit we have, I always come away feeling good and having learned something new.

He told me Monday morning that he was feeling some sort of calling of late—a calling to help others. He said he wasn't talking about just wanting to do some charity work, but he really was desirous of helping folks in need of serious help. Without saying so directly, he was grappling with a calling to somehow relieve others' deep suffering. He told me something I agree with wholeheartedly—that a person who himself has suffered in some way was in the best position to help others facing that same sort of pain. He wanted to use the pain of his past in a positive way of helping others.

To make his point, he started telling me about grapes grown on vineyards for wine. (His family owns a vineyard in Jamaica.) He told me that with grapes for wine, as opposed to those for eating or for just grape juice, it is often the vines that suffer the most that produce the best wine grapes. (To get technical on you for a turn, the smaller berries produce more skin, which contains more pigments, flavor, and tannins than the fuller, more pampered grapes.) My friend told me it takes a skilled vintner to recognize which of the "deprived" vines will produce the best wines.

When we parted Monday morning, I started thinking about our conversation. I started to think about how some of the most inspiring and beautiful people I know have suffered greatly in their lives. I thought of my own suffering and depression and how, in the strangest of ways, I feel blessed to have gone through what I have.

Often times human beings suffer from the lack of their most basic nutrients—basic kindness, love, compassion and forgiveness. Unfortunately this often leads to depression from which some of us never recover. On the other hand, some of us are lucky enough to have someone—a vintner of humanity, if you will—to recognize there's something left and patiently nurtures us back to health. (In my life, I know I have a personal vintner and she knows who she is. God bless you, Ann.)

For the sufferer's part, he has to recognize his self-worth, too. Yes, we often are subjected to a lack of nutrients. We are often beaten and crushed into submission—just like the grape. But then sometimes a wonderful thing happens. Sometimes we get an outpouring of the most beautiful and tasteful wine one can produce.

This is what I call the "wrath of the grape." Despite it all, and sometimes out of a vengeful or indignant kind of strength, we decide we have had enough, and we vow to become something of use, something beautiful and tasteful. (This is where I believe myself to be. Out of all the hurt, pain and suffering, I've made a decision to finally become my true self and someone I can be proud of.)

Finally, the real miracle happens. Sometimes we forgive and try our best to forget all the past. We experience the ultimate revenge. We place ourselves in a bottle of sorts and we age and mature. Then, one day, our truest nature and most beautiful self will be revealed.

I'm now in the bottle. I'm watching and learning. I'm aging and maturing. One day I will be uncorked and the best I have to offer will come pouring out. It hasn't happened yet, but I know it will.

I know my family is curious as to exactly what will pour out of the bottle that is me. It's a mystery to me, too, and I can't wait to find out. But no wine should be opened before its time. I've taken the steps I need to take thus far. Now we must wait. I am content to wait my time.

CONSEQUENCES

I'm reading a book entitled Rebel Buddha: On The Road To Freedom, by Dzogchen Ponlop. The author reminds readers that the Buddha's greatest teaching was in reminding us not to commit the error of not believing in cause and effect. Says Ponlop, such is "the epitome of delusion."

I am also reminded of each Catholic Mass where, as a group, all state, "I confess to Almighty God, and to you, my brothers and sisters, that I have sinned through my own fault—in my thoughts and in my words, in what I have done and in what I have failed to do." In effect, at every mass, each is reminded of the potential effects of all thoughts, words, deeds, and omissions. This is a powerful reminder to be cognizant of all aspects of our beings—from our mind as well as body.

Let's all try our best to keep in mind always the consequences of our very nature. Let's strive for pure hearts and minds. Let's strive for positive words and actions. And let's strive to refrain from harmful thoughts, words and deeds. Let us all be mindful that, like a mere raindrop, even the tiniest of deeds have consequences.

THE SUNAO MIND

"We do not want to be beginners. But let us be
convinced of the fact that we will never be anything
else but beginners, all our lives."

Thomas Merton

The other day, I heard the term "the sunao mind" for the first time. It was presented to me as a way of looking at everything all the time with an open mind and as looking at it for the first time.

As I do with most new concepts, I investigated a little further. Sunao mind is a Japanese concept with no direct translation in the English language. One of its most ardent practitioners is Konosuke Matsushita, the founder of Panasonic and Matsushita Corporation.

Matsushita defines it as follows: "Sunao mind is an untrapped mind, free to adapt itself effectively to new circumstances. A person with this mind looks at things as they are at the moment and colors them with no special bias, emotionalism, or preconception. A biased person sees everything through filters or a distorting lens... With Sunao mind one can learn from any source, anytime, any place."*

Indeed, the basic creed of The Matsushita Institute of Government and Management is as follows: "With a sunao mind, we firmly dedicate ourselves to the gathering of wisdom, the seeking out of the intrinsic nature of reality through independent study, and the searching anew every day for the path that will lead to new growth and development."**

To me, this is nothing short of a call to action each and every day. We must arise each and every day like the sun—undistorted by the clouds of yesterday. We must face each and every day anew—with a mind wide open—ready to learn all anew. In this way, all is learned for the first time each day, with no preconceived notions. We must force ourselves to be a child each day, learning everything as if for the first time. We then must apply our own wisdom (and nothing else) in interpreting our newfound knowledge.

PROGRESS, BUT WITH PATIENCE

"Be not afraid of growing slowly; be afraid only of standing still."
                                        Ancient Proverb

"Adopt the pace of nature; her secret is patience."
                                        Ralph Waldo Emerson

My nature is one of impatience. (I know, this despite my exclamation that I am content to wait my time as I said in my post, The Wrath Of Grapes. When I don't reach my goals on time, I get frustrated.)

I have come so far in the last two years. And believe me, I know how far I still have to go! But sometimes—well, a lot of the time—I just can't wait to see even more progress. Like all of us, I have so many plans for the future. I want to have the more loving and compassionate heart I have in my sight. I long for more wisdom. I long to live in such a way that each and every moment is one of peace. I can become angry waiting on tranquility!

We must all vow to work diligently at the tasks before us. And we must also realize sometimes the tasks are daunting. So we must be content to do our tasks with, and not against, the flow of nature.

We all must keep in mind that we are not Superman. We do not have the power to alter time or the course of the Earth. We are only human. No less, but no more. We must strive with our all—and that is a lot—but within limitations, whether imposed by our current weaknesses or by forces outside ourselves.

These are hard lessons for me to learn. But the good news is that I am learning my lessons—all of them. (A lot of them the hard way, still!) Whenever our patience is exhausted, let's try not to become frustrated to the point of standing still. Let's do what we can when we can, with the realization that, one day, we'll get there. We'll get there.

GO SLOWLY

"Never be in a hurry; do everything quietly and in a
calm spirit. Do not lose your inner peace for anything
whatsoever, even if your whole world seems upset."
                                        Saint Francis de Sales

"Nature does not hurry, yet everything is
accomplished."
                                        Lao Tzu

Years ago, I read an excellent magazine article on jazz musician Wynton Marsalis. The beginning sentence was, "Wynton Marsalis never gets in a hurry about anything." I don't now remember what magazine I read this in, or much else about the article, but I will never forget reading that first sentence and thinking about what a great trait that is, and how awesome it would be if I could cultivate this trait for myself.

Unfortunately for me, about the only thing I have not been in a hurry about is attaining wisdom. Like many folks, I have gone through my adulthood at an extremely hectic pace. As a young lawyer, I was taught that multi-tasking was the optimum. The more and faster I could cross things off my "to do" list, the better. "Time is money," I was often reminded.

Eventually the pace caught up with me and I faced burnout—in a big way. Along the way, I would think about Marsalis and the success he enjoyed—all while not being in a hurry about anything. But I did nothing but think about this and lament my situation. I didn't try to learn the secrets to Marsalis' success or how to live life in the way I imagined he did.

But, for me, the passage of time (and the blessings to have the support of my family), has afforded me the opportunity to address my situation. I've indeed learned to slow down. And, sure enough, I'm more productive now than I've ever been.

Let's look at the title of this post—Go Slowly. I think a lot of us would look at these two words and place the emphasis on the second—slowly. We read this message to slow to all but a halt, to be lazy or unproductive. But this is a mistake. Note that today's post contains an action verb—go—as its first word. We should always strive to be productive and make good use of our time and talents. Only next comes the adverb—slowly—which reminds us simply to be mindful of our pace.

The "go" in this post applies to all our actions—thoughts, speech, and other activities. How do we go "slowly" and at the same time be more productive? It's really quite simple. The Buddhist principles of mindfulness focus on doing one thing at a time—again, thoughts, speech and all other activities. This allows one to concentrate solely on the matter at hand and not be distracted by anything else. For example, if we are praying or meditating, we should strive to do only that and not allow other thoughts to intervene. In speaking, we should focus and strive to choose our words carefully and express ourselves in a kind and helpful manner. When eating, the goal should be to take time and enjoy the meal—and not do so while watching television or surfing the web. Simply put, by trying to do two or more things at once, we really accomplish nothing to our full potential.

Multi-tasking is contrary to accomplishing things in a mindful way. And rather than enhancing productivity, I believe it actually robs us of the ability to actually focus and accomplish our best. Any time we are doing more than one thing at a time, we are logically only able to devote a part of ourselves to any one of the tasks.

As the second quote above states, we could all learn something from nature. Natural law does not operate in haste. Yet all is accomplished. Every day lasts a full 24 hours—this is plenty of time to accomplish whatever we need to do. If not, we are simply over-committed and would be best served to look to make adjustments.

It's all very simple, really. We can go through life on autopilot and never really be mindful of anything. But if we do, we will miss out on so much—meaningful conversations with family and friends, a quiet ride home from work, wonderful meals, listening attentively to music, and many other things of importance.

Obviously it is up to you how to live your life. But I believe if you will try to "go slowly," you will find more meaning and you will enjoy life much more—all the while still accomplishing plenty.

LETTING GO OF NEGATIVITY

People deal too much with the negative, with what is
wrong. Why not try and see positive things, to just
touch those things and make them bloom?"
                                    Thich Nhat Hanh

"I've always believed that you can think positive as well
as you can negative."
                                    James A. Baldwin

For a good bit of my adult life—especially over the last 15
years or so—I believe folks would have summed me up by stating
that I am a "negative person." As ashamed of this as I am, I know in
my heart that this was an accurate assessment of me. I always saw
the glass as half empty, always looked at the dark side of things,
always emitted negative vibes.

Let me tell you a bizarre but true story. On and off for years,
my family has vacationed in and around Destin, Florida. During
our 2004 summer trip there, I went to nearby Seaside by myself
one day—just shopping around. I noticed a small tent selling
jewelry inside. I popped in to check it out. Immediately I noticed
an armed security guard, but no one else around. I began to look
at the expensive offerings.

Suddenly, out of the back walked a guy who looked as if he
was about to hit the beach for some surfing. He had very long, kind
of matted hair (the kind you get when you're just starting dreads),
and the only thing he was wearing was a pair of board shorts. No
shirt, no shoes, nothing. "Dude," he says to me, "you need to tone

it down—you sound like a bass guitar coming in here." I looked at him quite puzzled, as I had not said a word since entering.

He introduced himself as Sanjay, the owner of the place, and said I was putting off so many loud negative vibes that it was affecting his mood. He invited me to join him in the back. Intrigued, I followed. We walked into a tiny room, which was decorated in a rather odd fashion. His very bohemian girlfriend was there, seated in a chair to the side. Sanjay took a seat on a throne of sorts, in between two posters—one of Mary, the mother of Jesus, and one of the Buddha. He motioned for me to sit on the pillow in front of him. I took my seat.

Sanjay told me that, as soon as I walked in, he could sense deep negative vibes. He says he came out to investigate and found me. He asked if I was experiencing depression. I admitted I was. He told me basically to try to discover a way to "let go" and "lighten up." He said my negative energy was affecting my health. Then, before getting up, he said, "Hey, tell your wife that she will eventually find you." (I never mentioned to him I was married, but I'm guessing he noticed my wedding band.) That was it—the total of the conversation. I should have tried to engage him more, but I think I was just kind of shocked about what was happening.

We walked back out front and he told me to pick out something for my wife—"on the house." I picked out a kind of tropical looking bracelet and took it back to Destin and gave it to Ann and explained what had just happened. We were both kind of dumbfounded about this guy Sanjay and his ability to read me so well. Actually, it was one of the strangest experiences I have ever had!

Our family returned to the area in the summer of 2009. By then, we had been through some very difficult times with my depression. But in those five years, I had made a lot of progress and gotten quite a bit better. We went back to Seaside looking for Sanjay. His tent was gone. We asked around and some other merchants told us he had packed up recently and moved back to his home—France. Ann and I were disappointed as we wanted to let him know I was better, and Ann especially wanted to thank him for advising her (in his rather roundabout way) not to lose faith in me.

It's now 2011 and we are leaving again for the beach in a few days. We will visit all our favorite spots—we'll even look for Sanjay again, knowing he's probably not going to be there.

The main reason I really want to see him again is to find out a little more about him. To be honest, I didn't then, and still don't now, know what to make of him. I'd ask him—how does one read or feel vibes from afar the way he did? I also want to thank him for being so honest with me. He made me take a look at my life and what I projected to others. Finally, I'd want him to "read" me as he did before—so I could show him all the progress I've made.

If you are more of a negative type person, please ask yourself why. What reasons do you have for being so pessimistic? What is bringing you down? Life can be much better if you will simply make the decision to try to make it so.

I love the quote from James A. Baldwin above. It's so true—we can emit positive vibes just as easily as negative ones, if only we would try. And if we did, we would find that we would be happier and we could make those around us happier. (It's not just folks like Sanjay who can read people. All of us can sense negative vibes if those vibes are deeply intense.) We simply must vow to change our default setting from negative to positive. It takes time for this to become natural, but with practice, it can happen. And when it does, you can know a peace you have never known before.

As of now, I'm striving to lose all negativity. It's damaging to me and to others. It's also a complete waste of time and energy. It simply has no place in my being or in my orbit any longer.

How I wish I could find Sanjay and tell him the impact he had on me that day. I think he'd say something like, "Dude, good for you!" Being a man of few words, that would probably be it. I'm sure countless individuals have thanked him for his extra sensory perception and his willingness to be honest with folks about it.

Sanjay, wherever you are, I hope you are doing well. I hope you are continuing on your positive path and continuing to help others with your gift. Thank you for helping me.

NOTHING, EXCEPTING ACCEPTANCE

"Everything is what it is. And love is the only true path. There is nothing, excepting acceptance, to ensure peace will last."

Reg L. Carver

I used to be very materialistic. Whatever I wanted (and I wanted a lot!), generally I went out and bought. But a lot about me has changed. In terms of material possessions, I no longer own, or want, much at all. I have the basics and I've learned to live with that.

At times I do get down about not being able to afford the things I used to provide for others and myself. I'm human, and, like everyone else, I sometimes have dreams of owning something material—something I cannot have because I cannot afford it. When these times come, I try to remind myself that things are nothing more than that—just things. No material possession will make you happy—not one.

I came across a Bible verse the other day that spoke to me. 2 Corinthians 3:17 states, "For the Lord is the Spirit, and wherever the Spirit of the Lord is, there is freedom." This is so true and sparked my quote above. To learn to accept things as they are, and not as we wish them to be, brings freedom and is the mark of true wisdom and true happiness. Frankly, as the title of this post states, nothing, excepting acceptance of what is, will, or even can, bring you the freedom to be truly happy. But acceptance of God's spirit will bring real happiness. For God is in control, not us. By accepting what is, we are learning to let go of our own desires and accept those God plans for us.

I've learned this lesson so late in life. While chasing material possessions, I guess I was blinded to this truth. Thankfully I've at least learned it now. For now I know, I have all the possessions I will ever need or should ever really want—and that is the wisdom that God is in control and all I have to do is accept whatever is. Once you possess this most precious gift—this knowledge—you will find that nothing else really, really matters anymore.

I am human and I will never lose all want of material possessions. But I have come far. I have far more than material possessions now. Thank God for teaching me to humble myself to this truth.

PURSUING WISDOM
(WITH NO END IN SIGHT)

"By three methods we may learn wisdom: first, by
reflection, which is noblest; second, by imitation, which
is easiest; and third, by experience, which is the most
bitter."

Confucius

"We seem to gain wisdom more readily through our
failures than through our successes. We always think
of failure as the antithesis of success, but it isn't.
Success often lies just the other side of failure."

Leo F. Buscaglia

"The beginning of wisdom is to desire it."

Solomon Ibn Gabirol

These days, it seems I'm consumed with gaining wisdom. I
know that, in my experience, just the thought that I am pursuing it
makes me feel wiser and more at peace. But, the other day, it kind
of dawned on me that I really am unsure what true wisdom is. What
exactly am I pursuing here?

I turned to Dictionary.com for help. It defines wisdom as "the
quality or state of being wise." Okay, thanks, big help. I continued
my Internet search—mostly, in vain. I pulled up a lot of Bible verses,
but, to be honest, nothing seemed to provide me a definition of
wisdom and certainly nothing could describe a path to wisdom.
So, I've spent the better part of this week contemplating my own

thoughts regarding wisdom. I believe I have developed a personal definition and personal path.

First, as far as a definition goes, I would describe wisdom as "a state of mind where one consciously seeks to bring peace to any situation, to any group of people, and to oneself." Again, this is my own definition—I pulled it from my own thoughts alone. You are obviously free to accept it, reject it, or tweak it as you see fit.

Now, a trickier part—just what is the path to attaining and exhibiting wisdom? Again, I've relied on my own instincts here. But I believe I have developed a six-part strategy. I can only take credit for the particular compilation of ideas here. The thoughts and ideas themselves are not my own—again, only the particular combination.

So, here goes—my six-part path to gaining and exhibiting wisdom (as I define wisdom). As I love to do, I will begin each part with a quote that will hopefully make each component easy to remember.

1) Do not speak—unless it improves upon silence.—Buddha. This is one of my favorite components. How much of the time do we hear folks talk and, at the end of their remarks, we think things like, "that was not helpful," or "that seemed mean-spirited or combative." Moreover, it's been my observation that, most times, the quietest person in the room has the most meaningful and helpful remarks when he or she does speak. (It's kind of like barking dogs. No one pays any attention whatsoever to one that barks constantly. But, you let a mostly silent dog bark, and folks will perk up—something is going down!) So, please, be mindful of this. Choose when to speak carefully. And choose your words wisely.

2) Be kind whenever possible. It is always possible.—Dalai Lama. *This is another one of my favorites. And believe it or not, it is always possible to be kind. Even if we disagree with someone, we can do so in a way that is kind rather than harsh or involves personal attacks. (As a lawyer, I have seen countless disputes play out before me. I'm always mindful of the manner in which folks handle conflict. Believe me, the one who is most hostile generally comes out worse (certainly no better) than the one who exhibits kindness.) It bears repeating—kindness is always possible.*

3) What we see we become. Choose your seeing wisely.—Deepak Chopra. *This is very good advice. I know that there have been times in my life when I chose the wrong crowd with which to associate. I have also sought things that were not in my best interest. We must guard against associations that will hurt us in the long run. And, don't worry—you know—instinctively you know what is good for you and what is not.*

4) What comes from the heart, goes to the heart.—Samuel Taylor Coleridge. *This component speaks to the matter of giving and getting praise and criticism. As for yourself, always give both from the heart. For one, folks generally have an accurate BS radar—your praise or criticism will be seen exactly for what it is. Folks will appreciate either as long as it comes from the heart. The same goes for receiving praise or criticism. Keep your own BS radar up. And remember, receiving praise never really does you any lasting good—don't let it go to your head. And criticism helps only when given as constructive and from one's heart. If you are being criticized in any other way, simply smile and ignore it completely. Handled the right way, harmful criticism only harms the one uttering it.*

5) Do unto others as you would have them do unto you.—Golden Rule. *This one pretty much covers it all. I can think of no better way to sum up wisdom in dealing with others.*

6) Follow your heart.—*From the song, "Follow Your Heart" by Brett Dennen. When all else fails, you must simply fall back on instinct. And I believe we all are hard-wired to know what is wise and what is not. As long as your heart is in the right place (and you also know instinctively when it is or is not) just follow its lead.*

So, there you have it. This is, in my opinion, the best path to wisdom I can conceive on my own. Please remember that this is an endless path. You must strive to walk it every single day. But if you do, I promise you will know peace in your heart. And you will also help create peace in the hearts of others.

OVER AND OVER AND OVER—THEN AGAIN

> *"For a long time it had seemed to me that life was
> about to begin—real life. But there was always some
> obstacle in the way, something to be gotten through
> first, some unfinished business, time still to be served,
> a debt to be paid. Then life would begin. At last it
> dawned on me that these obstacles were my life."*
> *Alfred D'Souza*

This past weekend, I experienced difficult moments and emotions—the same ones that have plagued me as long as I can remember. It's insanity at its most basic level. When these times come, I ruminate on past events, past mistakes, the past in general—and it seems I only remember the most troubling parts of my past.

Today's post can be summed up by its quote. I've always been one to feel that my life would truly begin only upon reaching some milestone or other. It's been almost any phase—finishing elementary school, becoming "saved" as the Baptists call it, graduating high school, graduating college, graduating law school, making partner at the firm, finding the right meds, getting through ECT—you name it. I used to actually count to ten and then scream "GO" as loud as I could, thinking that at the point of "go," my life could then begin.

Yesterday I walked my dog, Annabelle, when I had the "urge to purge" and scream "GO!" But I stopped and smiled—I smiled that smile that comes when something finally makes sense to you. For the first time, it seems, it occurred to me just how many years

I've spent "waiting" to start my life. I think it finally dawned on me that I've been living now for almost 50 years. But it also dawned on me that every single day of my life—even every moment—could be an opportunity for renewal.

Truth is, rather than beat myself up over the past, I should just use it as a tool for improvement. And I should view each and every day as a fresh starting point. While I shouldn't view these starting points as the beginning of my life, I can view them as they truly are—the beginning of a new day or moment in time.

What I'm trying to say is that, no matter how much we wish it were so, none of us can erase or change our past. We experienced birth only once, and no amount of wishing for a new birth can bring it about. We must face reality about this.

But we can make changes—meaningful changes. And if we are sincere about making changes, one day we will realize we have come far. (Even now, I see evidence of this in my own life. Despite days like yesterday, I have made significant improvement. We should never discount our progress.)

Every morning as we wake, we should vow to make the day a good one. We should strive to be the best we can be that day. Each day will bring an opportunity to start fresh again. And we can use our past rather than deny it. Each new day we will be armed with our past (good and no so good) and the past can educate us on making the right choices in the days to come.

I've learned that life is most meaningful when we "embrace" rather than "erase." The former involves an acceptance of reality, where the latter seeks its denial. As the old saying goes, "the truth will set you free."

Please vow to embrace your life all your life. Acknowledge the truths of your existence. And then go out every single day and strive to be better. This is the most authentic way I know to live. Everything else involves something less than the truth. And there is nothing so powerful as the truth.

LET'S LOOK TO EACH OTHER

"I believe in the incomprehensibility of God."
                              Honore de Balzac

"In the faces of men and women I see God."
                              Walt Whitman

It seems the older I get, the more strongly I feel about two things: 1) that which is impossible for human beings to actually know is far greater than that which is possible to know; and 2) the folks who admit this truth have a far greater chance at finding a valuable measure of wisdom and peace than those who will not.

When I was going through my earliest stages of anxiety and depression, I was convinced that the one solution to my problems was out there—out there hiding somewhere. I was further convinced that there were learned people (clergy, doctors, or even sages) who could enlighten me. I viewed my job as simply finding the right person or persons who could provide the magic answers to my questions. I assumed that once I had completed this process, I could then simply follow their advice and I would eventually be cured of my ailments.

I went to see all kinds of folks—Christian ministers, Buddhist monks, psychiatrists, and, yes, even a guru of sorts. From some of these individuals, I was given very specific instructions—say these prayers this many times, read this particular text, take this particular medication. I was given advice on all sorts of matters and paths. (In one bizarre instance, I was even told by a member of the clergy that if I were to attend his particular church service every night for six straight nights, upon my death I would bypass "purgatory." Or, he advised me, if I wanted, I could designate someone who was already deceased and he or she would be released from purgatory immediately upon the conclusion of the sixth night's service! Yes, sadly, that's a true story.) With all these individuals, I found the least help. I learned eventually that, in general (though of course not always), someone who is cocksure of something generally hasn't a clue what he's talking about.

Among those I visited, I also was fortunate to find individuals who simply admitted that the key to finding peace and happiness is a complex endeavor—and that finding these ideal states sometimes can be a lengthy process—even lasting one's lifetime. I was reminded that each of us is unique (not only with our DNA, but with our particular set of experiences, triumphs and failures), and that the search upon which I was embarking is the most difficult one any of us can undertake. But these individuals also reminded me that the search could prove most rewarding as well.

Ultimately what I have found is that answers to my questions have been most easily found by a) trying to follow my own heart and soul, and b) just as important, if not more so, by simply looking at the way ordinary folks like me address life. I have learned to seek the counsel of my wife and my few friends. I have read many helpful biographies and autobiographies of people who have faced many of the same challenges I have. Through simply watching ordinary people conduct themselves in certain ways when confronted with various issues, problems, triumphs, and pains—situations and emotions that run the gamut—I feel I have seen examples of what works and what does not.

Most importantly, I believe I have often seen divine wisdom from others' triumphs and struggles. I believe God (or the divine, or natural law, or whatever you want to call it) finds a way of talking to us through each other. If we can be discerning in our observing, we can see God's wisest teachings every single day.

Talking to experts has helped. Taking my medication is invaluable. But nothing is better than finding answers and wisdom from others. God teaches us in the most simple of ways. To find guidance on much, we need look no further than to those with whom we interact every day. As the old saying goes, "some of are wise, and some are otherwise." We can learn a lot from each other. We need only take the time to see.

AVOIDING NOISE!

*"An inability to stay quiet is one of the most
conspicuous failings of mankind."*
                                       Walter Bagehot

"Nowadays most men lead lives of noisy desperation."
                                       W. S. Merwin

*"All noise is waste. So cultivate quietness in your
speech, in your thoughts, in your emotions. Speak
habitually low, wait for attention, and then your low
words will be charged with dynamite."*
                                       Elbert Hubbard

I like sound—sounds of all kinds. I like sounds of nature like the wind, the rain, and the singing of birds. I like the sound of good music, pleasant voices, laughter, and the whisper that is my dog Annabelle's snoring.

As much as I like sound, though, I absolutely despise noise (personally, I define noise as any sound that is both unpleasant and unnecessary.) As a matter of fact, I find noise one of the most bothersome things in life. And the problem is exacerbated by the fact that we are constantly surrounded by noise—and from an endless litany of sources—from the noise inside our own heads, to the constant chatter of machinery and gadgets that surround us every moment, to the completely useless babble of human beings. (The last one bothers me the most.)

I really started noticing all the noise in my life when I began to meditate. On the one hand meditation is a wonderful thing. But on the other, it highlights for me just how much noise surrounds us every day. Meditation has made me extremely sensitive to unpleasant and unnecessary sound. But such is life—"what are you gonna do?" as the saying goes.

Yes, the fact is, I must put up with noise. It's just a part of living in the world. But one thing I don't have to do is make noise myself. I can vow to make sure that, before making (or causing to be made) any sound at all, it will be either pleasant or necessary. I can also vow to make all sounds as quietly as is appropriate or helpful under the circumstances. (The only thing worse than noise is LOUD NOISE!)

I'm asking that we all strive to pay attention to our sounds. Are our sounds helpful, kind, truthful, and of importance? Or are they full of gossip, mean-spirited, meant to intimidate, or just simply of no value? Are we making good use of our voices, or are we hurting others (and ourselves) with them?

I ask that we all think about this sometimes. I believe if we did, we might find our interactions to be more pleasant, more helpful, or less combative. We might even find that some of our words are unnecessary and decide we can hold our tongues once in a while. We might actually contribute toward a quieter and more peaceful world.

Just think how nice it would be if most of the sounds we heard was something other than noise.

FINDING WHAT MOVES US

"Don't ask yourself what the world needs; ask yourself
what makes you come alive. And then go and do that.
Because what the world needs is people
who have come alive."
Attributed to Howard Thurman

It's simple, really. To have any chance at happiness in this life,
we must first ask ourselves what makes us come alive. As in my
case, it's mostly about finding wisdom and the pursuit of the arts
(and that includes the art of being oneself)—I guess creativity in
general. I know you can't afford to look back, but if I had it to do
all over again, I would have pursued a career in the arts in some
form—perhaps music, perhaps writing. But my life is not over yet.
I may find I can still pursue a path such as this before my days are
over.

So, as the quote says above, ask yourself what makes you
alive—what brings that tingling sensation in your chest and
head. It's there for us all; we just have to find it. And it can be

anything—math, science, sports, the spiritual, fashion, working with the disabled, building cars, or fixing motorcycles. But everyone is interested in something. (I'm reminded of what the Buddhist teacher Chogyam Trungpa Rinpoche once said, "everyone loves something, even if it's just tortillas.")

Think back to when you were a kid. What moved you as a child? It's likely that it is something that will move you to this day, and for the rest of your life—if only you will let it. Just think about it, try to remember, try to capture your heart before it became mired with responsibility and the muck that life becomes sometimes.

And once you have your answer, pursue it—on at least some level. Most of us will not have the freedom to quit our jobs and pursue our passions full time. (Some might.) But just do what you can. I think you'd be surprised how much difference it would make in your life just to have a hobby—an outlet that is pure love for you.

I'm moved now by many things—writing, thinking, and about taking the path that is true wisdom as I see it. Walking the path that is wisdom is an enormous challenge for me. I still have anger issues from time to time. I slip and manage to fall at least a bit almost every day.

But I'm not giving up this time. I know this now. I'm here for the duration. I am willing to do whatever it takes to become whole again. And let me tell you something—that is a beautiful feeling.

BECAUSE DANCING MAKES ME FEEL GOOD

I've always thought I have learned more from my kids than they will ever learn from me. And one lesson I will never forget resulted from the simplest of exchanges in the car while taking my oldest daughter, Caroline, to dance early one Saturday morning years ago.

Like most parents, my wife and I exposed our daughters to all sorts of activities from the get-go. We have tried music classes and piano, soccer and softball, the arts in general. In Caroline's case, she always participated with enthusiasm but didn't seem genuinely excited about any of it. We had the feeling she was going along just to please us.

But one day we bought a children's book about ballet. My wife and I would read it with Caroline at night before bed. Caroline announced out of the blue one day that she wanted to try ballet. We signed her up and began classes at a local studio. She loved it from the start—loved everything about it—the shoes, leotards and tights, her instructors, learning the language and techniques. Now 16, she's become quite a serious student of all the major dance forms, including ballet, pointe, modern, jazz, etc. She averages 15 to 20 hours of studio time on a weekly basis.

Back to the day in the car. Caroline had been dancing a few months by then. I'm taking her to the regular Saturday class and, just to make conversation, I asked, "Caroline, why is it that you like dance so much?" Without even a moment of hesitation, she smiles at me and says, "because dancing makes me feel good!"

End of conversation. We didn't say another word to each other the rest of the ride. I was dumbfounded by the wisdom of such a simple statement from a little girl.

I think that from the moment she laced up her first little pair of ballet shoes, Caroline knew she had fallen in love with something. She knew it in her heart and soul and knew that it was something of real meaning for her. While she could only express it then as "dancing makes me feel good," I believe she knew in her core that this feeling had intrinsic and undeniable value for her.

But what impressed me the most about all this is the wisdom she has exhibited since her beginning classes. Knowing in your heart that something of value makes you feel good is impressive. But she has gone far beyond that. At a very tender age, she dedicated herself to giving her all to dance and has never looked back. Not once have my wife or I ever had to remind her of a practice or to "step it up" or that we'd like to see her trying a little harder.

On her own, she's put in hard work to learn the very difficult movements and forms. She has, through her own efforts, auditioned for, made, and endured intimidating and intensive camps with the Joffrey Ballet and other professional organizations. She's learned to work through the nerves and stress brought about by the risk of literally "falling on your face" in front of audiences. Through it all, she's always risen to the occasion.

Caroline's efforts have paid off immeasurably. She has gained self-confidence, self-respect, and wisdom beyond her years She has gained many friends. She's learned lessons of discipline and they have paid off with school and other work habits. In sum, she knows now that giving your all to something you love is worth the effort. And as difficult as the effort is at times, the benefits always come back in greater measure.

I honestly cannot say I've given my all to much in life. But I believe this may be changing. I've been thinking a lot about Caroline lately. And because of some of the lessons I have learned from her, I see a lot of things differently.

WHAT WILL YOU SETTLE FOR?

Like a lot of folks, I began to follow professional golf when Tiger Woods joined the PGA Tour. But as I learned about the top players, it was David Duval who caught my attention most. I've always been struck by his modesty, his quiet demeanor (he usually lets his playing do his talking for him) and what seems to me to be his balanced view of golf and life. (Again, Duval has never been one to do a lot of talking to the media, but when he does, his statements usually strike me as being honest, open, and very intelligent and well reasoned. He has very interesting things to say and has a gift of saying a lot in a few words.) He isn't much on hype—despite some incredible feats, including scoring a 59 in competition, back to back PGA Tour wins, or twice taking the world's number 1 ranking from Tiger Woods—Duval simply keeps his trademark wrap-around shades on, signs his score cards, and quietly stays the course.

In 2001, in an interview after winning the British Open, he was asked about the hard work and struggle involved in accomplishing all he had. In response, Duval stated flatly, "I think, generally speaking, people tend to be as successful as what they will settle for." Upon hearing this, I remember thinking, "Wow—what a statement!" I wasn't really sure what he meant by it. And I didn't know whether I agreed with it. But in the ten years since, I've never forgotten his words.

I have probably thought about these words hundreds of times since he uttered them. What was he saying? Surely he was not saying that folks' success in life is simply or only a matter of what they settle for? Surely he knows that a person's lot in life depends on many factors—granted, one of them being his or her own desire and hard work—but surely he recognizes that other factors come into play, for example, economic circumstances and the chances one is given as a child, natural abilities and handicaps, many factors beyond one's control. How could he make such a bold statement as that?

Over this past weekend, I thought about his statement again. For what it's worth, I have finally concluded that I agree with Duval and I believe his words contain undeniable truth. But, as is the case with any quotation or statement, in order to really understand these words, I believe you have to look at the context in which they were made.

In reaching my conclusion, I believe David Duval was making a much broader statement than appears at first. You see, he could have just answered the reporter and made a specific statement about his own hard work in reaching certain goals he had set for himself as a golfer. But, notice that Duval, whether consciously or subconsciously, in response to the question about his personal golf achievements, simply lumps himself in with the entire human race. His response wasn't just about his own achievements. Again, he stated that people (I believe, referring to all people) tend to be as successful as what they will settle for. Duval was stating simply that, given his talents, as well as his resources for coaching and proper training, he knew he had the chance to become, at some point, the best golfer in the world. And he was stating that, given his circumstances, he decided he was not going to settle for anything less. He wanted to be the best he could possibly be at something that, at that particular time, meant the world to him. He wanted to be able to look at himself in the mirror and know he had given his all.

When taken in this context, what Duval said that day is absolutely true. For what he was really saying is that one's success is simply a measure of whether one has tried (or is currently trying) his best at climbing the mountain of his personal choice. You see, we all have talents and we all have limitations. We all have our own set of interests or aspirations. And we all look at success in different ways—some by the size of our bank account, some by the impact we make on the lives of others, some by the feats we accomplish in athletic or other endeavors. But one thing all people have in common is a way to measure our success—and that is simply whether or not we have given our all. Given the hand we have been dealt in life, how we play that hand and what we decide we will settle for is the true measure of our success.

So, at some point in all our lives, we must decide. Are we going to strive to be our true selves? Are we going to attempt to climb our mountain? And just what is the mountain of our choice and where is the summit for us? What will we give in our attempt to reach our personal summit? Will we give our all or will we settle for something less than that? In our own personal way, the sky really is the only limit. As David Duval stated (and as I can now say I unequivocally agree), each of us probably will be as successful as what we will settle for.

FEELING LIKE JefFREE

*"Within yourself deliverance must be searched for,
because each man makes his own prison."*
                                        Sir Edwin Arnold

Several years ago I would often go alone and hang out in a little section (just a few blocks) of in-town Atlanta known as Little Five Points (L5P). This is a very bohemian section of Atlanta. To put it mildly, I LOVE L5P!

The area is made up of lofts, funky little bars and restaurants, music venues, vintage clothing and jewelry shops, tattoo shops—you get the idea. A very open environment with little police presence, it is "live and let live" in Little Five. I love the people who hang there—you see a lot of unnatural hair color, lots of folks sporting dreadlocks, Doc Martens of every color—folks there are laid back in a big way.

I loved to mingle with the homeless and street artists. Sometimes I'd buy them lunch and we'd chat about all sorts of things. I loved talking to the musicians and visual artists. My favorite artist there was a cat named JefFREE—this is how he spelled his name. I thought it summed him up perfectly. JefFREE is indeed a free spirit and talented artist.

As much as I loved to visit, I was always depressed by the time I got back into my car and headed back to the suburbs where I live. The suburbs felt like a kind of prison to me. The suburban lifestyle represented a lot of what I didn't like. Don't misunderstand me, I loved being with my family (I knew they loved me—and probably even accepted me—and I knew I loved them dearly), but I just felt trapped in the northern part of Atlanta. I felt I didn't fit in my own neighborhood and community. I felt very disconnected to my neighbors and my co-workers. I felt no one really would accept me for who I am.

I felt I had to dress a more conservative way, and keep my mouth shut when the subject of politics or religion came up. I know my feelings were obvious to others, too. I never made attempts to really see the goodness of those around me. While I believed myself to be open-minded, I was in reality the most closed-minded person around. I created a prison in my own mind. I was miserable.

But a few years ago, things started to change for the better. I decided to attempt to just be myself and present myself as I wanted and just see what happens. I had fallen with love with tattoos and I got all I wanted. I decided to dress as I wanted as well. I was happier in my own skin, but at the same time was fearful others wouldn't accept me.

To my surprise, I was completely wrong about the anticipated bias and reaction of others. All my neighbors and community accepted the new (really just more authentic) me. My friends and neighbors didn't shun me at all. To my knowledge, folks accept me just the way I am. In turn, that has made me more accepting of others. I have myself become more open-minded.

I have learned important lessons in the last few years. Mostly, I've learned that my problems were simply my own and created in my own mind. Everyone noticed that, while I may have adopted a different look, I was still the same Reg they were initially introduced to. I was simply revealing my true nature and self. Honestly, it was I who was closed-minded. It was I who was the problem.

It just dawned on me the other day that I truly felt free to be who I really am, to look how I want to look, just to be me, really.

I thought again about JefFREE and smiled to myself as it dawned on me that I now feel as free as I imagined he did. I no longer needed to hide out in one section of town to be myself. I can be myself wherever I am.

This has been a humbling lesson for me. I don't like to admit that I was the closed-minded one, but it's simply the truth. Deep inside most folks are really open and accepting of others. You just have to give them the chance to show you that is indeed the case. I made the gigantic mistake of assuming folks were as closed-minded about me as I was about them.

Today I'm feeling free. I feel that priceless kind of freedom no one can take away from you. I live the best way I see fit and others accept that. Most folks (now including me) see right past outward appearances and see right to your heart and what's inside.

I'm glad and proud I have learned this lesson. I'm embarrassed it has taken this long. I'm so sorry I misjudged others the way I did. I will try to do better than this. Just like everyone, I'm a work in progress. But I'm making strides. I'm becoming truly free—free to be myself and free to allow others to do just the same. There's room for us all. There's no doubt about it.

LIVE THE LIFE YOU LOVE

"Live the life you love. Love the life you live."
                                    Bob Marley

You know, for so long I believed I suffered only from anxiety and depression. As these are both treatable ailments (and with all the treatment I have received), I couldn't understand for the longest time how I was not getting better. But now I see that, in addition to anxiety and depression, I also suffered from despair. And this makes a marked difference.

When we remain free from despair, we have not yet lost hope. We seek treatment because we believe there is a chance we can get better. But reaching despair makes everything much worse. Despair involves reaching the point where we no longer believe we have even a possibility of getting better. We can't even imagine a better day ahead.

At the time I was going through my worst periods, I could not see this truth about despair. And because I couldn't see it, I had no clue as to where to even start to get better. But, luckily, hindsight always provides a clearer lens.

You must know that despair is a vicious cycle. As long as you live in a state of despair, you absolutely will not get better. And it's a self-fulfilling prophecy. For as long as you believe there's no chance you can heal, you will find no point in trying to heal.

I want you to ask yourself if you've reached the point of despair. If not, try to see you are at least blessed in some measure.

And then start over by building on the hope of recovery. Hope is a powerful thing. A person can do a lot with hope.

But if you have lost all hope, let me suggest to you it is because you have completely lost your identity. I would bet you really have no idea who you are anymore. You no longer recognize yourself—at least on the inside. With despair, it's like someone you don't know has taken residence in your heart and soul.

With despair, a beginning lies in seeking to find yourself again. And the way to do this is simple—not necessarily easy, but simple. The beginning lies in asking yourself what you love (or once loved), what you are about (or used to be about), what moves your soul (or used to move your soul). And I'm talking about your deepest, most core beliefs, passions, and values. For if you find these places again, you will find yourself again. And when you do, you must resolve never to lose sight again.

I believe that we often lose ourselves due to the pressure (self-imposed or otherwise) to live as others expect us to. If we do this long enough, we will lose our true selves. For we cannot live the life someone else wants for us. We can only live our own life. Otherwise, we're just faking it. And, eventually, faking it will catch up to us.

Each of us is unique. We should live the life we were meant to live. We must not bow to pressure from others. (And contrary to what you might think, living only as others would have you live will actually bring you less respect, not more—from both others and from yourself.) In order to be fulfilled, to be at peace, and live with self-respect and the respect of others, we must live the life we love. We must love the life we live. To try to do otherwise will result in our not living at all.

If you have reached the point of despair, you must make a wholesale change. And that change first involves finding your true self—maybe for the first time ever. Don't despair. Just try. Try to be yourself—the most authentic form of yourself you can be. And you might just find that you will not only start to improve, you may actually find yourself reaching your authentic self. You might just find peace. You might just find a person you can love for the rest of your life.

FINDING OUR PLACE

"Some people are born to make great art and others
are born to appreciate it . . . . It's a kind of talent in
itself, to be an audience, whether you are a spectator
in the gallery or you are listening to the voice of the
world's greatest soprano. Not everyone can be an
artist. There have to be those who witness the art,
who live and appreciate what they have been
privileged to see."

Ann Patchett, Bel Canto

As long as I can remember, I've wanted to be either an acclaimed musician or painter. For a whole host of reasons, I didn't make it—and I'm pretty sure now that I never will. For the longest time, this bothered me greatly. I know many of you understand how frustrating it can be to go through life wanting to be somebody you will never be.

But I realize now that I have had much wrong the whole time. I've simply wanted something that was not meant for me. As crazy as it sounds, this really didn't dawn on me until reading the quote from Ann Patchett above.

Truth is, I can be an artist or musician—maybe not as I had first envisioned, but on some level nonetheless. I think I have a keen eye for visual art and design and a keen ear for music. I think I have a genuine talent regarding observation in general. I think my role in life may be in simply observing—and then reporting on that which I observe. If I fine-tune my observing to the best of my ability, maybe my writing can help others to see important truths—whether it is in art or life.

I feel blessed to have found my place. It means the world to me. And just like me, you have a place, too. The work involved is simply opening to whatever that place is. Please, take whatever time is necessary to find it. You will know it when you get there. And then hone your craft with all you have. The world needs you. The world needs everyone to give his or best.

Finding your place is the most rewarding accomplishment you could ever attain. Once you do, the world makes sense. Once you do, you can start contributing in ways no one else can. Finding your place frees you as nothing else can. It sets a fire that can never be extinguished. And all that is pretty cool.

raison d'etre

"Many men go fishing all their lives without knowing it
is not fish they are after."
Henry David Thoreau

"My heart is a gypsy—continuously searching for a
home, fighting within itself, wondering whether it is
weak or even right for that matter to be searching in
the first place. Loneliness is what it feels like . . . ."
Jenna Jameson

When I first enrolled as an undergraduate in college, I was
told I would be required to take two years of a foreign language.
I had never taken a foreign language before, so I set about trying
to decide on one. Having the mindset of a teenage boy, I decided
on French,—for the sole reason that I thought the French accent
was so alluring it might come in handy with girls.

French indeed turned out to be my hippest class. I remember
that my professor was from Paris—she was young and had the
coolest haircut I'd ever seen. Her accent was also as alluring as I
had surmised. I could have sat and listened to her talk all day.

I found French to be not terribly difficult to learn. Oddly
enough, however, I only remember a very few words—words
everyone knows like "bonjour," "au revoir," "oui." Sadly, that is
pretty much it.

But there is one exception—the words or phrase "raison
d'etre." In English this translates to "reason for being" or "reason

for existing." I always loved those two words together. I love the way they sound when pronounced with an authentic French accent. But also, I often find myself considering someone's (as well as my own) "raison d'etre." (And I wonder sometimes how, if asked, some folks would explain their reason for being.)

I love the two quotes above. (As an aside, who could have guessed you could cite the words of one of the greatest philosophers/writers of all time and an adult film star in the same article? And just for the record, I've never seen Ms. Jameson nude. The same goes for Mr. Thoreau.)

Thoreau's words ring so true to me. He reminds us that in everything we consider and do, we should question our purpose. As Buddha taught us, "what a man thinks, he becomes." It is always wise to consider our purpose regarding any action. Please, let us ask, "is it harmful or is it helpful."

Jameson's words are just as wise, but also cautionary. Like Thoreau, she reminds us to think about purpose. But her words consider more than just one's activities. She reminds us of the wisdom of questioning our very heart and soul. For if we don't do so often enough, we will find ourselves feeling lost and lonely.

Strive always to consider purpose—in your thoughts, deeds, and in the deepest part of your soul. It is time that is never wasted. And it could mean the difference between finding your way home and being adrift. The former is where the heart is, and the latter is not a good place for anyone.

NEVER, NEVER, NEVER GIVE UP

"When the world says, "Give up," Hope whispers,
"Try it one more time."
Author Unknown

The truth is, as much as I like to preach about not giving up, I in fact did—twice. As I saw it in my twisted mind and logic at the time, I felt I had failed beyond redemption. I saw no way to a better path. My suicide attempts were the most self-centered and cowardly acts I ever attempted.

But in another sense, I did not give up. For Ann carried me when I could walk no longer. She stepped in and didn't allow me to give up—even after all the pain, all the failures, and all the humiliation.

I'll never forget some things she said to me a few years ago now. (Ann isn't one to go around offering unsolicited advice.

When she did at this time, I knew to listen up.) It was around 2009 and I was in my phase of actually thinking of changing for good. I remember telling Ann that one thing that was holding me back was that in so many people's eyes, I could never overcome my failings.

She said to me, "Reg, you know, there's a lot to be said for just standing up. People often respect someone who continues to try—no matter what has happened."

Those words made a lasting impression on me. And Ann is right. I can think of many folks who have failed miserably in their lives, but stood up to take on the continuing challenges that make up a life. Why couldn't I do the same?

Ann also told me in a very direct way that my pride was holding me down. She reminded me that what others thought of me was really of no consequence. She reminded me that the most important people in my life were her and our daughters. And she made it clear that they all still loved me and would always stand with me.

At that moment, it really dawned on me how twisted my mind had become. She was right with every one of her points. It dawned on me then that almost everything I had done in my life, I had done for the wrong reasons. I felt really quite dumbfounded at that moment. "Wow," I remember thinking, "I'm late-40's, and my whole life has been built around things that were of no real consequence. I have missed the point of life entirely."

I remember thinking that I didn't want to waste any more time living in the realm of falsehoods. I wanted to get busy about the business of authenticity. I think this was a real turning point for me.

A LESSON FROM ANNABELLE

My family has never had good luck with dogs. Now, we've always had one dog or another—it's just that we have never had what anyone would call a "good dog." We've had a cocker spaniel that had one major health problem after another. We've had an English springer spaniel and German shorthaired pointer that both needed to be on farms where they could run as they were meant to. (We found more suitable homes for them both.) We had a yellow lab with such a bad case of separation anxiety that he ate through a metal crate while left by himself once. Our latest, "Buddy," another cocker spaniel, was so aggressive that he made no distinction between attacking adults and children alike. (We finally had to put him down before he really hurt someone.) We all swore that Buddy was it for us—we all knew it—as a family, we just weren't cut out for dogs.

Despite our pledge, as of this past spring (just weeks after Buddy's passing), we have a new dog. She's a 3-year-old beagle mix named Annabelle. We got her from a local rescue shelter one Sunday afternoon in May. Chloe, our youngest daughter, discovered Annabelle online and talked my wife and me into visiting the shelter to check her out. And you know what happens when you "just go look."

From the time we first brought her home, Annabelle has been nothing but a joy for our whole family. She's as sweet and gentle as any being could be. She loves everyone. She's always by one of our sides day and night. She is never a bother at all—she is simply appreciative of having a home and the love we all give her. I work from home and she and I are together most all day—she spends most days right beside my desk for hours. Whenever Chloe comes home from school, they are like two peas in a pod.

Annabelle has never torn up one shoe, one pillow, one anything. She greets everyone she meets with tail wagging and wanting a hug. She especially loves kids. Really, the only negative thing I can say about her is that she is the laziest dog on the planet. If movement is not absolutely necessary, she's not interested. (One exception—any treat involving bacon will bring a burst of energy equal to a shuttle launch!)

But what is really so special to me about Annabelle is the lesson I'm reminded of whenever I think of her. And that lesson is a simple one—"never give up." Annabelle would never have come to be a part of our family if she, Chloe, our other daughter, Caroline, or my wife or I had "given up." But the openness we all showed has paid off.

When we first visited Annabelle, the shelter volunteer told us that she was chosen for rescue from scheduled euthanasia for one reason—she seemed so sad in her holding bin. Folks said Annabelle just wouldn't and couldn't stop crying from the time she was brought in. They believe she had wandered off from her family and simply gotten lost. In her heart, Annabelle knew that life could, and was supposed to be, better and she was broken-hearted. She didn't give up on finding a new home and wanted someone to know how she felt. She did the only thing she could—she simply cried—cried with the hope that someone would hear her plea.

As for Chloe, she didn't give up, either. We had no more lost Buddy than she was on the lookout for a new dog. A friend told her about this rescue shelter's website and this is where Chloe discovered Annabelle. For several weeks, Chloe would pull up Annabelle's profile day after day and show it to my wife and me. Finally, we relented, to, again, "just go look." And finally, as for my wife and me, though we had been through it all with dogs, deep down we both loved them. We were open to giving the whole thing another try.

So, the lesson—never give up. No matter the dream or wish, never give up. As Annabelle knows, giving up on something important is the wrong choice and only ensures defeat. But by not giving up, you just might reach your goal. And sometimes that goal might be as important as finding a good home or the sweetest dog in the world.

LEARNING TO TRUST IN LIFE

"In three words I can sum up everything I've learned about life: It goes on."

Robert Frost

This week my youngest daughter, a middle-schooler, was given a Language Arts project of preparing a report about the life of a poet. She could choose one from a menu of seven provided by her teacher. Initially, she chose Robert Frost. She started her research and abruptly changed to Langston Hughes. I asked her why she made the change. "Dad," she said, "Robert Frost just had too sad a life. I can't deal with writing about him." I didn't know what she was talking about, so we researched it together. Turns out, I can understand exactly why an 11-year-old would feel the way she did.

Robert Frost (1874-1963), as you know, was an American poet. Indeed, he probably will be remembered as one of the most highly regarded poets of all time. In his lifetime he was awarded the Pulitzer Prize for Poetry four times. (That's right, four Pulitzer Prizes! How many folks have won one? Few indeed.)

Despite this success, his life was indeed plagued with loss. When just 11 himself (same age as my daughter), his father died of tuberculosis. Then only five years later, his mother died of cancer. At 16, he was left with no parents. In 1920, Frost was forced to commit his younger sister Jeanie to a mental hospital. She died there just nine years later. Mental illness seemed to run in the Frost family, as both he and his mother suffered bouts of depression. His wife, Elinor, was also a victim of depression.

Frost and his wife had six children and only two outlived their father. His son, Elliot, died of cholera as a child. His son, Carol, committed suicide in his 30's. His daughter, Marjorie, died of a puerperal fever after childbirth, and daughter, Elinor, died just three days after her birth in 1907. Frost's wife developed breast cancer in 1937 and died a year later of heart failure.

Upon reading all this, I could understand Chloe's sentiment. That kind of continual heartbreak is difficult for anyone to understand, much less a tender child. All week I have thought about Frost and the grief he must have endured in his lifetime. I also thought of how mine pales in comparison. I've had my share of hard knocks like anyone, but Frost seemed to have to bear way more than anybody's fair share.

Yet, Frost did not let his and his family's struggles prevent him from carrying his own life forward. I thought about the quote above, "it goes on." Indeed, Frost accepted this. But just what exactly did Frost mean by these three words. Like the meaning in the works of all great poets, I know his simple message must have had much deeper meaning than first meets the eye. He wasn't just saying that time continues to go by. I have tried to figure out what Frost meant with this little phrase.

I've come to a conclusion about his words and my conclusion has taught me a valuable lesson this week—and one I hope I will always try to keep in mind. I believe when Frost said of life, that "it goes on," he was reminding us that life does indeed endure, but that it does so on its terms and not ours. Frost learned this lesson early on and in a most personal and difficult way. Like nature, our lives take a course of their own, and, most of the time, we have very little control over the course of its events.

But there's a profound peace that comes from learning this most humbling lesson. If we can learn to accept life on life's terms and not our own (what a hard pill to swallow!), we can endure.

Through it all, we can endure—and endure in peace. For learning this lesson also frees us in a profound way. We will learn to stop the futile efforts at control and just "let it be." And when we do this and accept this, we can attain peace beyond even our own selfish expectations.

OBSERVING DIRECT CONNECTIONS

"Observe the direct connection between trust and the serendipitous events that follow."

Alan Cohen

I first read this quote a few weeks or maybe a month ago. I like it a lot. Ever since I first read it, I've tried to take it to heart. Let me tell you something. There is a lot of truth in this little bit of wisdom.

I've taken this quote to heart and observed it in my own life. I've been trying with all I have of late to let go of attempts at control. In all things, I've vowed to just trust what is and come what may. I've tried to believe in "trust." I have found that the more I follow this quote, the easier it has become to follow and the easier my life has become.

I've frankly lost count of the number of times over the last month that by simply letting to and ceasing efforts at control that I have witnessed serendipitous events unfold in favorable ways for me. This has been an extremely valuable lesson. If I will get out of my own way and let things unfold and hold on to trust (trust of others and of events in general), I will see that, as Bob Marley said, "every little thing's gonna be alright."

Please try this. Give it some time to prove itself to you. Even when things seem at first not to go your way, give it time to see that either a) it will have a way of bouncing back in your favor, or b) you can indeed be okay even if it doesn't.

At first, you may find this a difficult exercise. If you are like me, you might wish to revert to your default setting and attempt control. But keep yourself in check—just let it be. Continue to do this even if it seems illogical. Then just watch what happens.

This has been of immeasurable help to me. I want you to experience the same thing I have. Give this a little time and you will come to agree with me. You will find yourself enjoying this experiment as much as I do.

And sometimes, even the seemingly impossible will happen. Again, I've witnessed this firsthand over the last month. Please try to trust me on this. This is one of the best pieces of advice I've been given in forever. Free yourself to what is at every moment—just breathe—just wait—slow the mind—let go.

ALONE

"Loneliness is about the scariest thing there is."
Author Unknown

"Pray that your loneliness may open you into finding
something to live for, great enough to die for."
Doug Hammarskjold

I'm embarrassed to admit this, but so much of the time I feel so all alone. It's not because others are not there for me—they are. My wife, my daughters, my mother—they have been, and always are, there for me. They always are hoping for the best for me.

But I can't help myself. I feel unworthy. I feel unworthy of every good thing—of love, of friendship, of companionship, of even a smile.

I don't know what brings this about in a person. I really don't know that I will ever be able to put my finger on it. But when you feel it for a while, you know the most dreadful feeling in the world. And when you feel it long enough that it becomes a part of you, it never quite goes away. It gets better sometimes, but it is always there—that feeling that you deserve no one.

I keep living because I keep hoping I will find relief from the way I feel. I mostly pray for this because my wife and family deserve better. My family deserves better than I've given. I wish my family and I could experience better.

But you know what? I've been witness to miracles in my lifetime—real miracles. And I believe a miracle can happen where my loneliness is concerned.

So I continue to pray. I pray for relief. I pray for peace of mind. Mostly, I pray for those who have tried to help me along my way. For to see their happiness would mean more to me than anything in the world. When you know others have given their all for you, you really, really just want for them to experience the peace they deserve. That's what I want most. I want peace for those who have given so openly to me.

KEEP THE FAITH

"Without faith a man can do nothing; with it all things are possible."

Sir William Osler

"Faith is raising the sail of our little boat until it is caught up in the soft winds above and picks up speed, not from anything within itself, but from the vast resources of the universe around us."

W. Ralph Ward

Like everyone else, I experience the whole gamut of human emotions. Sometimes I feel hopeful, optimistic, and energized. Other times I feel anxious, upset, and angry. Sometimes I feel strong, and sometimes I feel I could use a shoulder to lean on.

Yesterday wasn't such a good day for me. Through the course of the day's events, I felt a measure of betrayal from two folks I would like to think are my friends. (Truth is, neither is a genuine friend—each is someone who calls upon me only when he needs help or if he can obtain a favor from me—but the very definition of a "fair weather friend.") Last evening, I became increasingly upset by these betrayals. It also affected my sleep and I still felt the stings this morning.

But, as I write this (it is early afternoon just before this post is going up), I no longer feel these negative emotions from just hours before. And the reason is due to a simple little text message I received a bit ago from my wife. The message was very short and very simple. Knowing how I as feeling, it said simply, "keep faith in humanity and in the Universe."

I really needed to hear that. You see, sometimes when something hurtful happens to me, it clouds everything else. I'm sure I'm not alone in feeling this way. But my wife's note reminded me of the basic goodness in humanity and in the forces of nature. In a gentle way, she reminded me not to let a couple unfortunate incidents dampen my spirit. I had to think about her note only a few minutes to feel the restoration in my soul.

It was Benjamin Franklin who said, "a man wrapped in himself makes a very small bundle." This is wisdom if I ever heard any. I must keep moving from the "I" mindset to thinking of the "whole." I know if I do this, I will remain on the right path.

THE WALKING PART

"Past the seeker as he prayed came the crippled and
the beggar and the beaten. And seeing them . . . he
cried, 'Great God, how is it that a living creator can
see such things and yet do nothing about them?' God
said, 'I did do something. I made you.'"
Author Unknown

Most anyone who lives to middle age has had to climb at least a few mountains. And, often times, we have had to carry heavy burdens in route. Ask anyone and you will be given the same answer—we were always grateful for the times we had help on our journey.

I believe life itself is much like mountain climbing. Even in the best of circumstances, just going the distance is difficult. Simply going through the motions—putting one foot in front of the other—is sometimes an arduous task. And when you add the inevitable surprises along the way (equipment problems, treacherous weather, crevasses), things can get very dicey very quickly. On the mountain—just as in life—you just never know what's ahead. Climbing alone is never a good idea. Everyone needs someone in walking the walk.

Of course, the higher the mountain, the more help that is needed. Most of us could handle Washington's Mt. Rainier (elevation 14,410 ft.) with basic support. But the highest one, Mt. Everest (elevation 29,035 ft.) requires a team of yak, Sherpas, and even supplements of our most basic life source—oxygen. Mt.

Everest is the climb of all climbs, requiring all the resources one can muster.

In life, most days we find ourselves facing Mt. Rainier. But at some point, almost all of us have to attempt our Mt. Everest. At these times, a good many of us make it. Some of us don't. One thing is for sure—our chances for survival depend a great deal on the amount of support we have along the way.

There will always be well wishers at base camp. And there will be many to offer praise if we reach the top. But the most crucial support is needed on the mountain. Unfortunately this is where we often find the least help. As the old saying goes, "a lot of folks talk the talk, but few actually walk the walk."

Are you a talker or a walker? If you've never considered the question, please do so. When you answer honestly, then ask yourself another—are you satisfied with the answer? If so, God bless you—the world needs both. If not, you need not waste another moment before getting busy.

SOMEWHERE AROUND "PLAN Y"

"Practice easing your way along. Don't get het up or in a dither. Do your best; take it as it comes. You can handle anything if you think you can. Just keep your cool and your sense of humor."
                              Smiley Blanton

"The world belongs to the enthusiast who keeps his cool."
                              William McFee

Today's post is a kind of reminder—to myself and perhaps to you. In fact, I need to be reminded of several things. I need reminding that I have a lot of faults. For example, I manage to find a way to take most things personally, am easily offended, make assumptions about folks' intentions where there is no basis in fact, and I do not handle personal relationships very well at all. The relationships issue is my biggest fault.

Now, I also am keenly aware of these faults and am very hard on myself about them. And my faults and then self-punishment cause me great pain. So today, I just wanted to remind myself to "ease up" and realize I can always give myself another chance—even if and when others do not, which, thankfully, is rare. If you struggle as I do, and benefit from this post, then I feel it has been worth my acknowledging these awful and embarrassing traits of mine.

Despite what you may be thinking at this point, this is not a "negative" or "down" post. In fact, it is the exact opposite! This post is a reminder of two things: 1) most folks are generous in

189

abundance with giving others second or more chances (thank the Lord); and 2) if other folks do not, you can always give yourself another chance. Always.

We have to trust in life—and the nature of life. We are not in control, and we certainly don't control our most basic make-up. Sure, we can, and should, work to improve ourselves—continuously—but we have to accept that we must work with what we have. We all have talents, sure, but we also all have faults. Rather than loathe ourselves for our faults, we should simply acknowledge them and try to do better. We must recognize that not one of us is perfect—and this is what makes us human. This is what makes being human such a special experience. Working toward bettering ourselves is what gives life its meaning.

In life, there are always alternatives and more chances. We just sometimes need help in seeing them. But with practice, we can. And we all need to learn—I mean really learn and know—the truth that alternatives and second chances always exist. Life is all about making mistakes and learning from them. If we expect perfection, we will only suffer disappointment.

All things in life—yes, all things—will work out and be okay if we let the natural flow of things just be. Ever consider that?—just letting the natural flow of things take their course, rather than trying to interfere. Believe me, if you will just have some measure of trust (as Jesus said, trust that is no more than the smallest seed—the mustard seed), I assure you that you can learn to accept yourself (with all your faults) and know that you are a beautiful person—or at least a beautiful person in progress.

I try to control. I try to run interference. I try to be something better than I really am. But let's relax. Let's just trust ourselves. Let's trust that we are good enough. Then let's watch what happens.

"IT ISN'T SUPPOSED TO BE LIKE THIS"

"The snake which cannot cast its skin has to die. As
well the minds which are prevented from changing their
opinions; they cease to be mind."

Friedrich Nietzsche

The moving story of renowned mathematician John Nash and his wife, Alicia, as depicted in the 2001 film, *A Beautiful Mind*, made a significant impact on Ann and her unwavering support of me. The movie tells the story of a mathematical genius destined for greatness, but who falls victim to schizophrenia. The movie leaves one with the impression that but for the unwavering support of Alicia, John Nash would have never healed.

Ann first saw this movie alone on an airplane. She told me that, in watching it, she thought over and over that our situation was very similar. Ann told me she knew I was sick, and she felt that she was the only person who could make me see things differently.

She vowed to never give up on me. As she has put it many times, "it just isn't supposed to be like this."

Ann has been there for me since she was just a teenager. We had our hopes and dreams. We married—and I now know she meant it when she said, "for better and for worse." I've given her more of the "for worse" than anyone, especially she, deserves.

Ann has been through it all with me. She had to watch my downward spiral. She has stood by me during all my trials with medication. She went to ECT with me every day. She never saw me as a failure, even as I did. Even when I fell flat on my face in business, she just said, "hey, it's just not you. Let's find something that is." Ann always has offered a smile and a hug and said, "it's going to be okay." And I know she has meant it every time she has said it. You see, Ann never lost faith in me. She never gave up on me. Not once.

It's not the least bit of a stretch to say that I would not be alive today if it weren't for Ann. She is bringing me back to myself. She is showing me the way. I thank God every day for Ann.

DEVELOPING COMPASSION

Compassion is a word thrown around a lot these days. When we witness tragedies like those in Haiti and the recent troubles stemming from the oil spill in the Gulf of Mexico, news outlets speak of the "outpouring of compassion" for those in need. Indeed compassion has been used so much of late that I thought it a good time to look at my own thoughts on the word and revisit what it means.

Dictionary.com defines "compassion" as "a feeling of deep sympathy and sorrow for another stricken by misfortune, accompanied by a strong desire to alleviate the suffering." As I look at this definition, I am immediately struck that it has two parts. The first part is the "feeling of deep sympathy and sorrow." Like most folks, I think I feel sympathy and sorrow for others quite naturally and quite often. To me, this is just a part of being human. Indeed, recent studies at the University of Wisconsin, Princeton University, Emory University, and the University of California, Berkeley all suggest that humans are hard-wired for compassion.

For me, the more challenging aspect of compassion is the second part of the definition—the "strong desire to alleviate the suffering." I need to cultivate this second part of my nature. Others have done it. In Chasin' the Trane, his excellent biography of jazz great John Coltrane, J. C. Thomas noted that Coltrane was "so thoroughly attuned to the sensitivities of the human soul that he suffered all his life from a melancholy as profound as Shakespeare portrayed in his character... [named] Hamlet." When I read this I always wish I were not so self-centered and could develop this level of compassion for others.

But I'm going to try. I'm going to try for two reasons. First, I'm going to try because it would be the right thing to do. I can think of no greater purpose for myself (for all of us) than to set about each day with a goal of helping to alleviate someone else's suffering. And I don't think this has to be some grand or global undertaking. As Mother Teresa said often, "in this life, we cannot do great things—we can only do small things with great love." I need to work on these small things. I need to smile more, look out for my family and friends more, my neighbors.

The second reason I want to develop compassion more fully is to simply help myself. With my anxiety and depression, I am seemingly always concerned with myself and how I feel. I believe if I would focus more on helping others, I would find I would be less consumed by my own feelings. My mind could be occupied with other pressing matters—being kind to, and helping, others. I believe this would go a long way in helping me to heal.

YOU ARE NOT ALONE

When you suffer from depression, you physically hurt sometimes—can be often times. Your head hurts—whole body, really. You are exhausted and literally feel like anvils are piled on top of you. But most of all your heart aches and you feel all alone. It seems everyone else is enjoying life and making their way just fine. You, however, feel trapped with your stomach in knots and not able to move. These are the feelings when depression hits the hardest.

You are not alone. I promise you this much. I'm with you—I'm thinking of you. Others are, too. You may not feel like it, but at any given moment, you have a whole lot of folks thinking about and praying for you. Lots of us have suffered too many of these same days. And for those of us who have, despite how good we may feel today, the demons may be back as soon as tomorrow. And we'll be in the same boat.

For me, when the worst of the days used to come, they would set me back for weeks or longer. I couldn't seem to shake a bad day for the longest time. And I know it's because I felt so alone. I felt that somehow depression had chosen to visit me and me alone. While everyone else in the world was living, I was dying inside—breathing, yes, but essentially dying. These were the worst of my times. You may be going through these times right now. If you are, know that I feel for you and am hoping you will feel better soon.

But how to feel better? It's simple, but not easy. The simple part is to just hold on. Just vow to hold on for at least one more day. And it's easier to hold on when you accept one of the

Buddha's greatest truths—"everything arises, and everything falls away." Indeed, if you will commit to waiting out the sorrow and pain, it will eventually pass. It won't last forever.

Hang on. I will be thinking of you. Please know that you are not alone. You were happy at least once in your life—remember that—and you can be again. Summon every ounce of strength you have and vow to turn all that negative energy on its head. Call or visit family or a friend if at all possible. If not, get up and find something positive to do—find something that inspires you and spend some time with it. Stay with it until the depression begins to lift. It will—eventually it will.

FORGIVENESS—SELF AND OTHERS

In healing from depression, for me, one of the most significant aspects of the process involves forgiveness—forgiveness of self and others. Like everyone else, I am only human and I have made plenty of mistakes in my life and have caused pain to others. Conversely, others have harmed me. I have found that perhaps the most significant impediment to becoming whole is in my inability or unwillingness to forgive. Moreover, out of plain old guilt, I have found it difficult to accept the forgiveness of others. But we have to get beyond this.

Self-forgiveness involves accepting yourself as a human being who has faults. It also is letting go of anger for your past failures, errors, and mistakes. Finally, it allows for self-love after you have admitted your failure or misdeed.

Of equal importance in healing is the forgiveness of others. An excellent resource is the website www.forgivenessandhealth.com. In it, Judith Perlman notes "as a psychotherapist specializing in health psychology for over twenty years, I've come to understand that in order to live fully and joyfully in the present, it is absolutely necessary to release the pain that we all carry with us from the past . . . . Without the power of forgiveness to help us heal, the past has the potential to destroy our present lives. Giving up the pain of the past is not easy—but is one of the keys to a healthy life."

Over the last year, I personally have worked very hard at self-forgiveness and the forgiveness of others. The benefits to me have been nothing short of a miracle. People around me, people who know me and see me on a daily basis see this, too. I'm coming to know peace—peace I have never known in my life. Please give forgiveness a chance to work miracles in your life.

AT LEAST YOU KNOW

I'd say the worst of my anxiety and depression lasted somewhere between six and seven years. This is a lot of time. And quite a bit of damage was done—to me, to my family, my friends. By now, the worst of the damage has been healed or far along the path toward healing. That's the good news. But the opposite is also true. There is damage that is yet to be resolved—and may never be resolved. I'm talking here about personal relationships.

Recently, I posted on the topic of forgiveness and the role of forgiveness in healing. (Forgiveness—Self And Others). I discussed the importance of forgiving self and others in order to heal. I can honestly say that I have tried my best to forgive myself for the harm I caused others. I can also say that I have truly forgiven everyone for any harm done to me. This has brought me peace in great measure.

I'd be lying, though, to tell you that I'm totally at peace with the whole forgiveness issue. One thing I didn't discuss in my previous post was how I feel about those who have not forgiven me for past mistakes. In other words, the previous post dealt totally with the act of forgiving. I did not address the notion of receiving forgiveness.

For the longest time, I dwelt on the notion of how great it would feel if everyone would forgive me for my misdeeds. Not receiving forgiveness of some has caused me emotional turmoil. And the funny thing is, it's those I've harmed the most who have wholeheartedly forgiven me. It's those on the receiving end of my least transgressions who hold continued grudges. But I've learned that I must accept this and move on.

I learned this lesson from a dear friend. We had gotten to know each other over the course of regular lunches and cigars. We always talked about a lot of things—we covered a lot of ground—mostly fun topics like travel, family, and food. But occasionally we would talk about serious matters—health issues and the notion of happiness.

About a year ago, during the course of one long lunch/cigar get-together, the subject of my anxiety/depression came up. I mentioned that I felt in order to really heal, I needed others to forgive me. Upon hearing this, he responded immediately that it was absolutely necessary for me to try my best to forget about this. He reminded me that I did not (and could not) control others' decisions regarding forgiveness. And then, he said the most interesting thing of all—he told me, with respect to those who wouldn't forgive me, "Reg, at least you know." He told me I'd find peace in that knowledge.

I didn't quite know how to react to this revelation. I didn't understand how in the world I would ever understand it, either. But, with the passage of time, I've come to understand that my friend is exactly right. I cannot control whether others choose to forgive me. And he's also right that just acknowledging and knowing this in my heart has brought a measure of peace.

I'm reminded of a passage in Anthony Bourdain's latest book, Medium Raw, where he writes of the difficulties brought about in trying to straighten out from past mistakes. Says Bourdain, "[f]acing 'reality' after a lifetime of doing everything I could to escape it offered no rewards that I could see. Only punishment. No solution presented itself. I couldn't go back (that way blocked for sure), and I couldn't go forward . . . . And I was angry about that. Very angry." (For what it's worth, Bourdain explains later in the book that his efforts have since paid off and he is now at peace.)

The wisdom of my friend's lesson (and which I also learned from Bourdain's book) is clear to me now. I have had to learn to let go of the need to control. If certain folks won't forgive my mistakes—well then, so be it. I know now all I can do is simply continue to walk the path that is life. Others don't live your life—only you can live your life. Continuing to pine for others to forgive me is a waste of mental energy.

Sometimes I still feel like I'm walking a lonely road, but I'm moving forward nonetheless. Today happens to be my birthday—and it feels good to be walking in peace.

COOLING THE FLAMES

Unfortunately, we live in a world of violence. History teaches us that this has always been the case. And as long as human beings inhabit the world, we probably always will. But that doesn't mean we should just settle for the status quo, doesn't mean we should just accept our world as is and never try to improve its state. Just as we try to improve anything else, I believe we all have a duty to devote consistent efforts toward improving the human condition—within ourselves, between family members, in our local communities, even globally.

Violence takes many forms. Of course there is physical violence—from one person to another person or being, or from a person to some sort of object. But there are also many other forms of violence—emotional violence within our hearts and souls, there is violent language, and there is the violence of passive aggressive conduct. Indeed, violence is a broad topic and cannot be adequately addressed in one blog post. But I do want to address one aspect of violence and offer one simple observation on helping curb some forms of violence.

It seems obvious to me that most, if not all, violence stems from some form of anger. And I believe that the root of this anger is in a person's feeling that he or she is not being heard. Or, even if being heard, I believe a lot of folks are made to feel that their feelings or opinions are not worthy of our attention. I believe that when folks feel they are not really being heard, they are more apt to lash out—and some of this lashing out is taking the form of harsh violence. In turn, this violence is resulting in severe consequences to all beings—from the person being violent to his or her targets.

So let me offer today one simple observation to stem violence. Let us all vow to try to be better listeners. Let's listen to our own hearts first, and then let's listen—really pay attention and listen—to our spouses and partners, our children and our parents, our friends and neighbors, our teachers and students, our colleagues, and all members of our community. Let's strive to take the time to listen to one another. And once we've listened, let's offer the best we can in response.

In his wonderful book entitled Anger, Thich Nhat Hanh echoes this sentiment much more eloquently. Says Nhat Hanh, "To understand and transform anger, we must learn the practice of compassionate listening and using loving speech . . . . Listening with compassion can help the other person to suffer less . . . . Listen with only one purpose: to allow the other person to express himself and find relief from his suffering. Keep compassion alive during the whole time of listening. You have to be very concentrated while you listen. You have to focus on the practice of listening with all your attention, your whole being: your eyes, ears, body, and your mind. If you just pretend to listen, and do not listen with one hundred percent of yourself, the other person will know it and will not find relief from his suffering . . . . Compassionate listening is a very deep practice. You listen not to judge or blame. You listen just because you want the other person to suffer less."

Please strive to be a compassionate listener. All beings everywhere will benefit from your commitment.

LOVE AND A HOME

"I feel that there is nothing more truly artistic than to love people."

Vincent van Gogh

"I wish they would only take me as I am."

Vincent van Gogh

Vincent van Gogh (1853-1890) has always been one of my favorite artists. In the late 1980's, I visited New York City for the first time. I spent a day at the Metropolitan Museum of Art and, at the time, there was a special exhibit of his work during his time in the psychiatric wards in Saint-Remy and Auvers-sur-Oise in France. Throughout his entire life, van Gogh suffered from severe melancholy—I've read of diagnoses of depression, bipolar disorder, and temporal lobe epilepsy. With psychiatric medicine what is was at the time, I don't know that we'll ever know from which malady he really suffered.

I absolutely loved the bold colors with which he painted. But as much as I love his art, I fell in love with Vincent, the man, even more. For his entire adult life, van Gogh was consumed with the idea of relieving the suffering of others. In one of his many letters to his brother, Theo, van Gogh noted that the best medicine for anyone was "love and a home." And what I've come to believe that van Gogh really meant by this was that, more than anything, human beings need to feel a part of a family.

Knowing of Vincent's fragile psyche, Theo provided his brother with financial support his entire life. Nevertheless,

Vincent always felt estranged from his family and felt no one really accepted him. Indeed, at one point in his life, he felt a calling to the ministry, but ultimately failed in his attempts to complete his work at the seminary at Vlaamsche Opleidingsschool near Brussels. He did serve as a missionary in the village of Petit Wasmes in Belgium for a time. There he lived among the peasants he ministered to, taking residence in a small hut at the back of a local baker's house. He was filled with such compassion for the poor souls that the baker's wife was said to be able to hear van Gogh sobbing all night in his hut. His squalid living conditions were not acceptable to church officials and he was ultimately dismissed for "undermining the dignity of the priesthood."

Fortunately, he ultimately found his true talent and calling as a painter and we are blessed to have so many of his works to now admire. Despite that he must have known how truly beautiful his works are, van Gogh was never able to shake his melancholy and his feeling of rejection from his own family and nearly everyone he encountered. I believe that Vincent van Gogh never felt truly loved by anyone. As we all know, van Gogh died of suicide in the wheat fields he painted so vividly.

This past week was a celebratory one for our family. Each night we watched our daughters perform their annual Spring dance recital and chorus concert. I thought a lot about van Gogh this week. I thought of how fortunate Ann and I feel to have the family we have. I hope our daughters always know how loved they are by Ann and me—indeed by many extended family members and friends. With all my problems with depression, I always knew my family loved me. I always have had a loving home in which I was a part. For that, I am truly grateful.

Vincent van Gogh was right, the best medicine for us all, ill or not, is "love and a home"—family. If you are fortunate enough to have family, rejoice, for you are blessed. The best you have to offer is love to your family. But this doesn't only include the traditional family of mother, father, and children, and extended family of grandparents, aunts, uncles, cousins, etc. No, this includes the whole of the human family—the whole of the human race.

Please remember that we are brothers and sisters. Please also do not fail to remember that many of us feel we have no family. Many feel rejected by all of society. This is the most awful feeling I could imagine. We can all help by loving each other. Please offer your love to no less than every single person you encounter—you may have no idea what battle he or she is facing. Sometimes, it is the smallest act of love—a smile, a hug, a compliment, or the smallest favor—that will make all the difference in a person. Sometimes it might just mean the difference between life and death.

FOR THE LEAST OF THESE

BROTHERS OF MINE

*"The King will reply, 'I tell you the truth, whatever you
did for one of the least of these brothers of mine,
you did for me.'"
Bible—Matthew 25:40 (NIV)*

Yesterday afternoon, I ran into a situation I have been in many times. It's the same situation many of you have experienced—especially if you live in a large metropolitan area.

My wife, youngest daughter, and I are all seated at a very casual restaurant, enjoying a late lunch. Like a lot of Americans, we'd been awake about six hours—and we were already working on our second meal of the day.

Out of the corner of my eye, I noticed a pleasant, petite woman—probably mid-thirties—walking with a child. The two were approaching each table and the lady handed a card to someone at each one. I knew immediately what was happening. Again, I've seen this many times. And this time was, sadly, like all the others. Before reaching my table, each person to whom she handed the card simply handed it back and nodded his or her head with an emphatic "no." (Some were on laptops or had headphones in their ears, and they didn't so much as give the lady the time of day.) Each time, the woman and child took the card back and proceeded to the next table.

When the lady approached us, she handed me a card that read something like this—"I am from El Salvador. I have 2 kids and I lost my job. I need money to buy food." I read the card as I was pulling out my wallet (with a picture of Bob Marley embossed on it!), and I handed the lady a contribution. She didn't smile, she just looked a bit relieved and whispered to me, "God bless you."

Silence hovered over our table. My wife, daughter, and I all felt that lump in your throat just before having to fight back a tear. We didn't say a word to each other for several minutes. Finally, my daughter, Chloe, asks, "so Dad, what did the card say?" I told her, and reminded her of the Bible verse quoted at top. Chloe couldn't find any words. It's difficult to see that reality—up close—for the first time. Well, truth is, it is always difficult to see.

As the whole thing went down—over and over at each table—I went through the gamut of emotions I always do. First, I feel horrible that I live in a world where folks are hungry to the point of begging. Next, I am angered that so many folks just turn away. Finally, I am so pleased to give—it's not about the money to me so much as I want the person to remember that at least one table of folks took the time to acknowledge her as a human being and gave something. I always feel honored to show someone that there are still people in this world who care.

Chloe finally broke the silence again, asking, "Dad, why doesn't everyone give her something?" I said, "well, Chloe, I really don't know. It's someone's right whether to give or not. Some folks think she is just running some sort of scam and doesn't really need the money for food. And some folks just don't give money to strangers." Again, silence. I could see the wheels spinning in her mind about what her response would or should be. She never let me in on her thoughts.

I have seen this so many times I have lost count. When I'm with a group of folks, a lot of the time I will be ribbed about being a sucker for giving the person money. They sometimes give me advice, and say something like, "he's just going to buy alcohol or drugs!" or, just directly, "man, don't give to them!" And you know what? I will bet that sometimes, maybe many times, my companions are correct. Yes, I will bet that more often than not, I have indeed been "scammed."

Honestly, I am just fine with that. You know why? Because I will also bet that there have been occasions where I have not been scammed. I will bet that there have been a few occasions where I looked into the eyes of a brother or sister and helped someone in real need. Yes, maybe just a few times, but I know in my heart it's happened. And that makes every time I am made a fool completely worth it. Honestly, the only regret I ever have is that I don't have more to offer—that may sound pious, but it's the honest truth.

Let me ask you this. When you are approached by someone asking for help, would you rather feel superior because you have not been swindled, or would you rather take the chance you might actually be helping someone? The answer is simple. The answer depends solely upon the size of your heart. I ask you, how big do you want your heart to be?

TAKING REFUGE

"Peace comes from within; do not seek it without."
Buddha

After leaving the Christian faith, I vowed to never join another organized religion. And I haven't. But what I never have abandoned is my belief in God and the continued cultivation of my spirit.

I came to explore Buddha and Buddhism through my interest in the Trappist monk Thomas Merton. I discovered Merton's writings long ago, and I think he is one of the most brilliant men who ever lived. Late in his short life, Merton began to take interest in Eastern religions, including Buddhism. And he became friends with the Vietnamese Buddhist monk Thich Nhat Hanh. (Dr. Martin Luther King, Jr. nominated Nhat Hanh for the Nobel Peace Prize.)

I read a lot of Nhat Hanh's works. The more I studied them, the more beautiful I found the Buddha's philosophy to be. I put my toes in the waters by attending the Shambhala Center in suburban Atlanta. I learned to meditate. And I started studying Buddhism in earnest.

I think what attracted me so much to Buddhism is the simple but profound wisdom it offers. In my opinion, everything one really needs to know about Buddhism can be summed up in the Buddha's two most basic teachings—The Four Noble Truths and the Noble Eightfold Path. If you apply yourself and really understand these teachings, and put them into practice, it will change your life in profound ways.

The Four Noble Truths are the foundation of Buddhism. In a nutshell, the first of these truths is that life is suffering. ("Suffering" as used by Buddha means suffering as we commonly know it—pain, illness, aging—as well as changing. So when Buddha used the term "suffering," he simply meant that all things are constantly in a state of change.)

The second of his truths was that the cause of our suffering is our attachments to certain states of being. In other words, we attach ourselves to, and strive for, whatever it is that brings us pleasure, while at the same time trying our best to avoid anything that is not pleasurable. Our lives become a constant struggle to alter what actually is, and to try to make it as we want.

The third truth is the good news. It is that we can avoid all this suffering. And, finally, the fourth noble truth tells us how. We do this by doing two things: 1) learning to accept life on its own terms—in other words, accepting what is; and 2) by following what the Buddha called the Noble Eightfold Path. This path is a basic guide for living, which calls for right view, right intention, right speech, right action, right livelihood, right effort, right mindfulness, and right concentration.

This is the essence of Buddhism. As I said, with some amount of in-depth study of The Four Noble Truths and the Noble Eightfold Path, anyone can benefit from the Buddha's philosophy. And the most beautiful aspect of Buddhism of all is that anyone—I mean anyone—can become Buddhist without it interfering with or contradicting anyone's other religious or spiritual beliefs. Buddhism does not take a formal position regarding many things—the existence of God, the existence of an afterlife, the existence of Heaven or Hell. The Buddha left it up to each of us to investigate these matters and decide for ourselves. Literally, you can be a Christian, Jew, Muslim, agnostic or atheist and still consider yourself a Buddhist. (That's "worldwide open" and that's what I'm all about!)

As I stated, since leaving the Christian faith, I have not formally joined any other organized religion and I do not expect I ever will. I have taken the Buddhist Refuge Vow, which is simply a vow to take refuge in what is known as the Three Jewels of Buddhism—the Buddha, the Dharma (which are the Buddha's teachings), and the Sangha (which is the Buddhist community). But I have not joined any particular "school" of Buddhism and have not joined any temple. I simply follow the wise teachings of the Buddha as I understand them. And Buddhism has been one of the greatest blessings of my life.

I'M NOT SHAVING MY HEAD

A few years back, I took the Refuge Vow and formally committed myself as a Buddhist. Living in the Southeast, you just don't run into many Buddhists. And for most folks I see on a day-to-day basis, they have no clue about Buddhism (despite that it's the fifth largest of the world's religions), and really have no desire to learn anything about it, either.

Honestly, this bothers me a little bit—well, it bothers me a lot sometimes—so much so that I get uncomfortable in conversation if the subject of one's religion comes up. The times I've been asked directly, "What religion are you?" and I say, "I'm Buddhist," I get that puzzled but positive look, then an "Oh," sometimes followed by "cool." And I know what their first thought is—"Wow, Reg worships Buddha—not God, but a hulky stone statue." Inside their heads, the eyebrows are rising big time, and they're thinking, "I wonder if he's going to be shaving his head?" At this point, the religion conversation ends and it's on to something more comfortable—the person is thinking, "Geez, let's just move on to some common ground here."

From time to time, I'm going to use this blog as a way to explain a little about Buddhism. There are just certain things I want folks to know about my chosen religion. I really want people to realize that Buddhism is a beautiful and wise philosophy for life.

Just who was Buddha? Well, I believe that, first and foremost, the Buddha would want you to know that he was an ordinary human being, just like you and me. Born Siddhartha Gautama about 2,500 years ago, he was a member of a royal family from a small kingdom, which was part of what is modern day Nepal.

Beginning in young adulthood, through a lengthy process of many trials and tribulations, and much meditation, Gautama became enlightened—he found the way to end the mental and emotional suffering that most of us experience on a daily basis.

Upon his enlightenment, he was given the title of the "Buddha," meaning "the awakened one." He spent the rest of his life (he died at age 80) explaining to others the philosophy and practices that freed his mind. He never held himself out as God (or any type of supernatural being), and never asked anyone to worship him. As a matter of fact, he asked people not to take his advice on faith alone, but to try his methods for themselves, and if they found something better, then to discard his teachings and go with their own.

The religion of Buddhism takes no official position on whether God exists. It's up to each practitioner to decide on his or her own about this. Thus, Buddhism does not prevent me from believing in the same God/Creator I always have—the same God I believed in when I was a Christian. As a matter of fact, Buddhism has actually strengthened my faith in God.

I am proud to call myself a Buddhist, but I don't worship Buddha. I respect Buddha and his teachings deeply. And I will for the rest of my days.

RULING THE MONKEY MIND

In noting the tendency of man's thoughts to wander erratically, the Buddha stated once that the untrained mind was like a drunken monkey being stung by a bee. And what an apt description! I know that, unfocused, my mind races from random thought to random thought—seemingly uncontrollably. And many of these thoughts can be intrusive and simply unproductive.

The polar opposite of the vision of the drunken monkey is the serene site of the calm Buddhist monk. Seated in lotus position, draped in a monastic robe, with a face still and completely composed, the monk reveals one state of mind—peace—not just a mind at peace, but a mind that is peace itself. Reaching this state on a consistent basis is a personal goal of mine. And I know it can be done. At the temple I attend occasionally, I regularly meet ordinary people who can do just this.

How do these people, with their brains no different than yours or mine, reach such peaceful states? And how do they seem to maintain these states of mind in the face of the same series of problems that make up life that you and I face? The answer is really quite simple. These people have trained their minds through mindful meditation—and they meditate regularly, like every day. The techniques used in meditation train the mind to focus at will. And a well-trained mind can keep intrusive or unwanted thoughts at bay at most all times.

Despite what you may have heard or believe, mindful meditation is a very simple practice. There is nothing particularly mysterious about it. Yes, it originated in the East, but is not limited to Eastern religious practice and will not interfere with any religious affiliation or practice at all. In truth, meditation has nothing to do with religion. (Granted, it might enhance your spirit or spiritual practice, as it will allow for enhanced focus. But this is just a side benefit—one of many that meditation will provide for you.)

Notice I stated that meditation was simple, but I did not state that it was easy. Much like exercise, to be beneficial, mindful meditation takes a genuine commitment and regular practice. Also like exercise, it will take some time before you will begin to experience noticeable benefits. But I promise that if you will commit to daily meditation for 30 days, you will see a substantial difference in your state of mind. Thereafter, you need only to continue a maintenance program that works for you.

Now, exactly what is mindful meditation and how do we get started? Mindful meditation is simply a technique of attempting to focus the mind on one's breathing for a certain period of time. (One usually begins by attempting 10 to 20 minutes at a time, then working up to what is comfortable and most beneficial.) You simply find a quiet, comfortable place to sit (usually on a cushion on the floor with legs crossed) and focus only on the sensation of your breathing. Try to notice your inhale and then your exhale—again and again—and try to focus on this alone. Undoubtedly, random thoughts will enter your mind. As you notice this, don't get frustrated, simply remind yourself that you are "thinking" and bring your focus back to your breath. Over time, you will notice that you are able to concentrate solely on your breath and nothing else for extended periods of time. The great benefit, of course, is that this is essentially training your mind to be able to focus at will and not allow intrusive thoughts to interfere.

I recommend that, in the beginning, you find a meditation instructor. (Many centers offer training at no charge.) If you do not have access to one, there are a number of books you can purchase which will get you started. (I highly recommend Real Happiness: The Power of Meditation, by Sharon Salzberg. The book includes an audio CD that is very helpful.)

I encourage you to check out mindful meditation. It has helped me get hold of my mind and I know it can be of benefit to you as well.

EVERYWHERE HE STEPPED

"As a lotus flower is born in water, grows in water and
rises out of water to stand above it unsoiled, so I, born
in the world, raised in the world, having overcome the
world, live unsoiled by the world."

Buddha

"You must be a lotus, unfolding its petals when the
Sun rises in the sky, unaffected by the slush when it is
born or even the water which sustains it."

Sri Sathya Sai Baba

Like any religion, Buddhism is full of symbolism. There is
the Buddha himself, tigers, dragons, the Dharma Wheel, bowls,
flags—you name it. Excepting the Buddha himself, my personal
favorite is the Lotus flower—it is so full of beauty, as well as a
metaphor for life and redemption.

I always have the Lotus flower on me. One of my favorite
tattoos is a beautiful orange/melon colored Lotus on my right
elbow. (That one was especially painful, but its beauty makes it
all worthwhile.) I wear a lapis blue wrist mala with a Lotus charm
attached.

The symbolism of the Lotus is beautiful. This flower, native
to Asia and Australia, is the national flower of India and Vietnam.
It is rooted in muddy slime, but works its way through water,
and finally blossoms while striving to reach the sun. In Tibetan
Buddhism, this is believed to mirror the journey of a man's soul.

The ancient story goes that, everywhere the Buddha stepped, Lotus flowers blossomed. I don't believe this to be factual, but simply a legend. It is instead a metaphor for Buddhism. The Buddha walked with such wisdom, truth, peace, and serenity that one felt his presence was as beautiful as a blooming Lotus.

Thinking about all this made me start wondering, "what is it that blossoms where I step?" I can tell you that it surely isn't the Lotus! For too long, it has been nothing more than weeds—the very definition of the most common of botanical life. I've grown into nothing special at all. I've never "blossomed"—only lasted through time and the elements. I've never even come close to having produced anything that anyone would deem beautiful. (Okay—two exceptions—I did have a hand in producing our daughters, two of the most beautiful beings walking.)

As humbling as my lot is, it also can be a wonderful challenge and catalyst for change—if only I would accept it. If I would just try, I'll bet I could transform those weeds into something more beautiful. Don't get me wrong. I know I'll never become the Lotus. But surely I can become something other than the common chickweed.

The truth is we all could stand to leave more beauty in our wake. Like the Buddha, we could walk with wisdom, truth, and peace at our side—we just need to give it the best we have. If only we tried, I'll bet we could have lasting beauty wherever we go. Who knows, maybe we could even sow a Lotus here and there.

THERE IS ONLY
THE PRESENT

"Life can be found only in the present moment.
The past is gone, the future is not yet here, and if we
do not go back to ourselves in the present moment,
we cannot be in touch with life."

Thich Nhat Hanh

I think the most important truth to remember about life is that it truly only takes place in the present. This is so simple it really needs no further explanation. There is really nothing to add to Nhat Hanh's quote.

That said, living in the present is one of the most difficult things I have ever tried to do. I have made slow progress. And I guess I can be proud of that. But if there is only lesson I need to learn over and over, this one is it.

WORRY

I'm a worrier—have been all my life. I remember as a child, my father always telling me, "Reg, you're going to worry yourself to death!" I will worry about anything—you name it, and I have some deep concern about it. Once, during a therapy session, my psychiatrist asked, "Reg, is there anything you don't worry about?" I responded, "well, I don't worry that tomorrow I'm going to wake up and discover I'm female, but everything else is fair game."

One bit of good news for me—I don't believe I've passed my worry genes to my children. (I've of course worried about this, too.) On my oldest daughter's Facebook page, she notes—"Don't worry about anything. Phil. 4: 6-7." Maybe my daughters will grow up to be well-adjusted people in spite of dear old dad.

The sad truth is that 1 in 4 Americans suffer from an anxiety disorder sometime in their lives. As the old Chinese saying goes, "the mind is man's best friend or his worst enemy." And to add insult to injury, worrying is completely useless. We all know this.

But the effects of worry can be debilitating. Excessive worry can cause a whole host of health problems, including, among other things, fatigue, nausea, head and muscle aches, and insomnia. At its worst, it can lead to coronary artery disease and heart attacks. The Indian philosopher Krishnamurti put it beautifully, "if your eyes are blinded with your worries, you cannot see the beauty of the sunset."

So, if we all agree that worry is useless and debilitating, how can we stop it? Recent studies agree that there has been much progress of late in treating anxiety and worry—even the most severe of cases. And some of the most effective treatments are simple things anyone can do.

Regular exercise is a great stress reducer. Any exercise will help. I heartily recommend yoga (especially Bikram Yoga) and walking/running. Meditation can also help train the mind and provide one with the tools to keep unchecked worry at bay. Prayer helps, too. If you are so inclined, offer up your worries in a prayer to God. (I have a verse tattooed on my arm—"Come to me all you who are weary and burdened, and I will give you rest. Matt. 11:28." For me, it helps to look at it sometimes and remind myself to just let go and let God take control.)

Another way to combat worry is to connect. Try to stay connected with family, friends, classmates, and colleagues. Being alone is a real danger for the worrier. With no one around to help keep the mind occupied, it is free to roam into dangerous, negative territory.

If the above doesn't help, you may need professional help. Excessive worry (the kind that can interfere regularly with your ability to live your life) may be a symptom of a serious disorder, like OCD (Obsessive Compulsive Disorder), GAD (Generalized Anxiety Disorder), PTSD (Post-Traumatic Stress Disorder), and could lead to panic attacks. If this might be your case, please consider consulting your physician. All these ailments are treatable and there are many types of therapies available, including simple talk therapy up to a wide variety of medicine and other treatments. You and your physician/therapist could decide and work through the best course of treatment for you.

Worry is useless and unnecessary. But it seems to be becoming a greater problem now more than ever. If you think you need help, you probably do. And you are never going to be able to focus on finding peace and happiness until you can commit and get your mind under "control." Truth is, you simply won't have the stamina to stay focused on the positive if you are trapped in the negative. Don't stay beholden to worry. Please get the help you need.

BROTHER TRYING TO CATCH A CAB

Years ago, I flew all the way from Atlanta to San Francisco just to hear Branford Marsalis in concert. (This was in the days I was flush and could afford to do something so spontaneous.) I had to go. He's one of the best tenor saxophonists out there and his trio at the time consisted of Jeff "Tain" Watts on drums, and Reginald Veal on bass. This was some seriously good jazz music.

He opened with "Brother Trying To Catch A Cab (One The East Side) Blues" from his 1992 album, I Heard You Twice the First Time. Marsalis did not disappoint. He captured the blues sound and feeling perfectly with that number. That saxophone wailed a plaintive sound like I'd never heard played live. (I've heard the same type sound many times listening to John Coltrane's recordings, but there's something really special about hearing the sound of feeling blue live.)

The last few days I have felt really blue inside. Work has been especially stressful. Family life is really busy right now. I'm feeling anxious inside. I need a break. But you know what? I now call these my "exam" days. These days are like taking a school exam. They are a measure of how much I've learned of late. A measure of how well I can handle the challenges before me and the feelings of anxiety, the feelings of rejection from others, the feelings that no one cares.

I pass these exams now more than I used to. But it's still hard—I'm not going to lie. It's still hard. But I'm learning that we all have days filled with the blues. Looking at them as exam days helps. Learning to laugh at these days helps, too. One thing that is especially helpful is in knowing these days will pass. They will. You just learn to go ahead and let the blues work its number on you. You take your exam and see how you did. You give yourself a grade.

And then you move on to tomorrow. Maybe you'll have another exam day, maybe even the dreaded surprise of a pop quiz. But maybe all will be as cool as though you have a substitute teacher—no pressure on those days. Who knows? You just take it one day at a time.

SMILING AT FEAR

Dictionary.com defines "fear" as "a distressing emotion aroused by impending danger, evil, pain, etc., whether the threat is real or imagined; the feeling or condition of being afraid."

It has taken me my lifetime to realize that the root of all my problems with depression is fear. The fear of what? The unknown. And the fear of the unknown came (and sometimes still comes) from my inability to exert control—control over outcomes, people's reactions, many things.

I have finally figured out that, as I am only one human being, there is very, very little that I am actually in control of. (There are a few things. For example, I can control to a large degree my efforts at something. I can also control how I choose to respond to a given situation—with compassion, sympathy, or anger, for example. And it's very important that I do pay attention to what I can control and give my best in these situations.) But the simple fact is, however, that a lot is simply out of my control. There are just too many factors that go into any given situation.

With my newfound knowledge, one would think that I would now be fearless. Knowing I control very little should, in theory, make me fear very little. Hey, there's very little I can do to avoid an inevitable uncomfortable, painful, or dangerous situation, so I should have no fear, right? Probably so, but I notice that I still have a good bit of fear lurking in my mind. Honestly, I deal with some kind of fear every day.

But there is good news. I have learned to deal with my fear in a way that takes away most, if not all, its potency. Put simply, I've learned not only to face my fears, but, in fact, I've learned to smile at fear.

What do I mean when I say smile at fear? Through the Buddha's teachings, I've learned mechanisms for taking the power away from fear. By facing fears instead of running from them, I've reduced their powers over me. Noted Buddhist teacher Sylvia Boorstein perhaps puts it best, stating, "the gesture of fearlessness is a simple gesture of accepting whatever is . . . . This 'whatever' is the whatever of truth. Things happen because other things have happened. Karma is true. This is what's happening in this moment. It can't be other than this. This is what it is, and the truth is always soothing. Fearlessness also comes from benevolence and goodwill in the face of whatever oppresses you. You are afraid, but instead of fighting what faces you, you embrace it and accept it—you develop loving-kindness as a direct antidote to fear."*

Another way I've learned to smile at fear is to realize that most of my fears are rooted in the future and never actually materialize the way I envision them. I have wasted so much present time in fearing what may materialize in the future that it really is a shame. Mostly, it's a shame because rarely have my fears actually manifested themselves in the exact way I imagined. And, importantly, when faced with a tragedy (one anticipated or not), I have always found the strength to deal with it in some way. Moreover, often times, someone has always been there to help and I have almost never faced my difficulties alone.

I will never lose all my fear. I think that's true for us all. (Now, there is the possibility that, during my lifetime, I will become totally enlightened and reach Buddhahood. I know. Those of you who know me personally and are reading this are saying to yourselves, "Reg, you—reach Buddhahood? It's just not going to happen, brother." I'm afraid I agree.) But I have learned the important lesson of smiling at it. Like a schoolyard bully, fear is not nearly as menacing as the mind makes it out to be. Often just standing up to it and smiling can weaken it substantially. And once in a while, it can even be enough to render it completely powerless.

*   www.shambhalasun.com—Fear and Fearlessness: What the Buddhists Teach

RADICAL TRUST

*"No one can really pull you up very high—you lose
your grip on the rope. But on your own two feet you
can climb mountains."*

Louis Brandeis

This past Wednesday evening, I was feeling very down and depressed. My wife was away on a business trip. When she's away, I almost always fall into a bit of a funk. Most days I am alone as I work from home. It's just my beloved companion, my dog Annabelle, and I during the daytime hours. But I know Ann will be home at night and I always look so forward to that.

So Wednesday night late, I am feeling a bit lost. In a weak moment, I posted on Facebook that I felt lost and wanted to hear from anyone who cared. This was a mistake—one probably shouldn't post something so personally deep on Facebook. Initially, it only got worse. I received only a handful of comments. To be exact, it was six, but two were folks who simply hit the "Like" button of my status of feeling lost! (Are you kidding me?)

But two of the most helpful bits of advice I got were from folks I only know though this blog. One was from an Australian lady who reminded me simply to "breathe." Darn good advice and I did do a bit of meditation, which helped.

The most moving piece of advice I got was from a lady in California. She says, "taking you into my heart, Reg, and holding you there in love and joy, knowing that feeling lost for a bit often

237

leads to great and wonderful transformation. Radical trust my friend."

I cannot explain in words how much that meant to me. She showed me great compassion and also offered the wisdom to use my feelings as a time for personal growth. My friend did all she could do from so far away. She wanted me to know she was thinking of me, but at the same time, she wanted me to get to work for myself. Finally she reminded me I must rely on radical trust that things would get better. What a beautiful gift I received from her thoughts and words.

So, as I said, I initially thought my posting was a grand mistake and was embarrassed by it the instant I touched "Send." And I can assure you I probably won't post something so drastic again. But out of that blunder came a beautiful message.

I am reminded of some important things from this little episode. First, I am reminded of the importance of compassion and the showing of compassion. We must strive to develop compassion and we must also not be hesitant to share our compassion. For just seeing my friend from afar's concern brought me hope at a dark hour.

Also, I was reminded that it is I and I alone who is responsible for my peace of mind and happiness. I must develop the tools and skills for finding my own joy. No one can, and no one will, do it for me. It's simply an impossible task to ask of another.

The message that sticks out to me most is the two simple words—"radical trust." I really needed to hear that and I must diligently pursue my ability to let go and trust. I must trust that all is okay in this moment, and that all will be okay in the future. I must be mindful to live in the present moment, knowing that nothing is permanent and all (including the times when I'm low) will indeed change.

WHEN WE FEEL OVERWHELMED

"Man performs and engenders so much more than he
can or should have to bear. That's how he finds that
he can bear anything."

William Faulkner

"I know God will not give me anything I can't handle. I
just wish that He didn't trust me so much."

Mother Teresa

In his wonderful book, The Road Less Traveled, M. Scott Peck, MD begins by stating of the greatest truths I know—"Life is difficult." Indeed, those three simple words impart more wisdom than contained in the whole of some books I've read. And no one is exempt from this truth. All of us find life difficult—even overwhelming—at times.

What are we to do when faced with those most difficult or overwhelming times? I believe there are several things we can do—from the very simple to more involved solutions. We should first remember this, however—for every problem there is a solution. Whether we admit it or not, deep inside we have the capacity to manage whatever comes our way—one way or another. The key is to trust in life and always strive to face our difficulties head-on.

Allow me to suggest a few things we might try when feeling overwhelmed. I have learned that these things help me and I am hoping they prove helpful to you as well.

When faced with any problem, I believe the first thing we must do is really ask ourselves what is the reality of the situation. In other words, step one is to identify the real problem. Why are we feeling overwhelmed? Are we stressed out over a personal relationship? Are we over-committed or feeling unorganized? Are we facing a financial crisis due to loss of employment or severe illness? Whatever it is, we must initially take the time to think through the root of the problem. In this way, we can at least identify the dragon we must slay.

Step two—we must breathe. I know this sounds simple, but if we can just take a moment and breathe, it will help clear our head and heart. Turn off all distractions—the radio, TV, our cell phone. Breathe quietly and calm yourself. A clear head makes for optimum decision-making.

Step three—we must thaw or loosen ourselves. Sometimes we can literally be frozen by fear and this prevents us form taking appropriate action. I am reminded of one time while looking at my dad's high school yearbook. Under his senior picture was a quote from him—"I'm scared stiff, but it's a great feeling." This was the voice of a young man in 1955 about to face the world as an adult. And with no parents to guide him, my dad was in a very real sense alone. He was excited to begin making his mark as an adult, but he admitted he was afraid of what he faced. Sometimes, we are simply afraid of the unknown.

Step four—take action. By now, we have reminded ourselves that we can face come what may. We have clearly identified our situation, we have focused, and we have thawed. It's time to really do something about our situation. Can we handle it on our own? Will a simple apology do? Can we make a "to do" list and just start plowing ahead? Do we need assistance? Should we seek professional help? We must answer these questions and get busy. Plugging away, one step at a time, we can get through anything.

Always face a problem or difficulty head on. To only treat parts or symptoms of a problem without getting at the root only delays continued pain. Also, we must ask for help if we need it. We should not be shy about seeking advice from family and friends. Sometimes just discussing our situation with one we trust can get us moving along the road of recovery.

Obviously, there are many different types of problems and different degrees of difficulty with any situation. But I truly believe that these small steps will at least help in identifying our situation and beginning the process of resolution. Please remember, there is nothing we cannot endure. We must trust this.

MATTHEW 6: 25–34

"Therefore I tell you, do not worry about your life,
what you will eat or drink; or about your body, what
you will wear. Is not life more than food, and the body
more than clothes? Look at the birds of the air; they
do not sow or reap or store away in barns, and yet
your heavenly Father feeds them. Are you not much
more valuable than they? Can any one of you by
worrying add a single hour to your life? And why do
you worry about clothes? See the flowers of the field
grow. They do not labor or spin. Yet I tell you that not
even Solomon in all his splendor was dressed like one
of these. If that is how God clothes the grass of the
field, which is here today and tomorrow is thrown into
the fire, will he not much more clothe you—you of little
faith? So do not worry, saying 'What shall we eat?' or
'What shall we drink?' or 'What shall we wear?' For the
pagans run after all these things, and your heavenly
Father knows that you need them. But seek first his
kingdom and his righteousness, and all these things will
be given to you as well. Therefore do not worry about
tomorrow, for tomorrow will worry about itself. Each
day has enough trouble of its own."
                    Bible, Matthew 6: 25–34 (NIV)

The above verses from the Bible are taken from Jesus'
"Sermon On the Mount." In that one sermon, Jesus sets forth
enough wisdom to hold one in good stead for his or her lifetime.
And the ten verses excerpted above really are nothing less than
the whole of how one should live his or her life.

Let's take a look at these verses. In the first three, Jesus reminds us of the futility of worry and that God will take care of all creation, from man down to all other animals and plant life. For the sake of our peace of mind, we should all try to rely on this truth.

As you look at the following verses, Jesus clarifies this further, assuring us that God understands our needs and promises that God will do right by us. Jesus also reminds us, however, that there may be a condition to being able to rely on this promise. For Jesus states that we are to first seek God's kingdom and his righteousness—and then all will be provided for us. Now, to be honest, this both frightens me and provides me with assurances.

How is it that we seek the kingdom of God? What exactly is God's kingdom? I'm no Biblical scholar, for sure, but I believe Jesus is saying that man is required to take care of all of God's creation. We are stewards of the Earth and should strive to protect it and all its inhabitants. Next, Jesus reminds us that we must seek righteousness. I get this one. This is a reminder to strive for wisdom in all forms—love, compassion, kindness, being nonjudgmental and being forgiving. Again, I'm no scholar, but this is my opinion of what Jesus is saying.

As I stated above, this frightens me somewhat as I have not always been a good steward of God's kingdom and I have not always sought righteousness. But I do believe in God's unconditional love, compassion, and forgiveness. I believe God will give me (and anyone else) the chances to correct my ways. And I believe God understands man's fallibility and is always willing to give us chances and new life. Every day is a chance to begin anew in seeking God's kingdom and righteousness. I believe that.

God will provide all that we could possibly need. And as Jesus said, we can just look around at nature to see this in action. There is simply no need to worry. No need to worry about anything. But with these wonderful gifts come responsibilities. If we live in such a way that our hearts and minds instinctively tell us is right, we are seeking the Kingdom of God and righteousness. We must strive to take this responsibility seriously as this is all God asks in return. Simply being loving, kind, compassionate, nonjudgmental, and forgiving in our daily lives is not too much to ask. Really, it is God's way of giving us a gift. For by doing these things, we will find our best and truest selves. And we can then soar—in the best of times and even amidst our darkest hours.

LESSONS FROM 9/11

*"I do not want to foresee the future. I am concerned
with taking care of the present. God has given me no
control over the moment following."*
                                    Mohandas Gandhi

All this month I have been watching documentaries and news programs about 9/11. I find it all riveting. I have questioned myself as to why this is and I have come to conclude it's because I have been so inspired my the stories of those who endured so much—the stories of bravery, the stories of hope, the stories of rebuilding. I have also learned valuable lessons from 9/11 and I wanted to share four of them with you.

One—We Have Little Control. Despite what we may think, to a person, each one of us has very little control over the future. We cannot control the thoughts and actions of others. We cannot control the weather and natural disasters. We have very little control whether we will become seriously ill. Whether we like to admit it or not, this is an irrefutable truth.

On one hand, this can be very unsettling. We like to be in control of things. Not actually having much control is difficult to accept—especially for those of us who are "control freaks." But, then again, this can be very freeing. We never know what is around the corner. Sure, any future moment may bring heartbreak, but it also may bring abundant joy and happiness. We must learn to embrace the present—the only thing we have—and take the future as it comes.

Two—Everyone And Everything Is Vulnerable. We may not feel it, but everyone and everything is constantly vulnerable to any circumstance under the sun. Ten years ago, almost no one could even fathom that the World Trade Center buildings could become dust within minutes. But, as we all know, it happened.

And we are all vulnerable. No matter who you are, you are vulnerable to any number of tragic events. There is not much we can do about this, either. Sure, we can recognize this and take steps to reduce the chances of tragedy. But ultimately, we all must remember that no one is immune from what we would deem tragic. Accordingly, we must seize each day as it could be our last—for one day we will be right!

Three—Attitude Is Everything. In watching all the television programs this month, I have been awed by the attitudes of those facing danger and loss. From the stories of the heroic first responders, to everyday folks helping others, and to the local and national figures who showed leadership, I have been reminded that our attitude makes all the difference in the face of tragedy and difficult times.

Sure, we do not have much control over events. But one thing we certainly have—we have control over our attitude toward, and reaction to, any event or circumstance. And we must realize that a positive and helpful attitude is always the wisest choice. (I know this personally—in my heart. But honestly, I struggle a lot with this. This is the one lesson I need to learn the most—and learn it over and over again.) Because of the bravery and calm demeanor of so many, a good number of lives were actually spared on 9/11. And many who sustained devastating injuries (physical and emotional) have been able to reach some measure of healing as a result of their positive attitudes.

Four—We Can Rebuild. No matter the situation in which we find ourselves, we can rebuild. I think of so many folks who have rebuilt from tragedy—folks who lost entire families in the Holocaust, and folks like Sen. John McCain, a POW in the Vietnam War for years, those who lost much yet have worked so hard to rebuild in New Orleans, and our brothers and sisters in Japan who recently suffered unspeakable tragedies from a tsunami. I could obviously go on and on. The point is that many have shown us that we can rebuild—no matter what. It may take everything we have, but we can do it.

Sadly, tragedies will always come—from those affecting only one or a few, to those affecting thousands of lives. It's inevitable that we will all face them. This is a truth we cannot control. But we can meet our tragedies with wisdom, and we can learn from them, and we can rebuild—at least in some measure. The only tragedy from which we cannot recover is that of giving up. Strive to never give up.

REAR VIEW MIRRORS

"When I am anxious it is because I am living in the future. When I am depressed it is because I am living in the past."

Author Unknown

"Looking back you realize that a very special person passed briefly through your life—and it was you. It is not too late to find that person again."

Robert Brault

I am obsessed with my car's rear view mirrors. Practically every time I begin driving, I do so by adjusting all of them. I even installed tiny circular mirrors that fit within the regular mirrors on the sides! Yes, this is the truth. I fear having even the smallest of a blind spot. (By the way, I've decided there are two categories of people who buy these tiny mirrors—a) those with obsessive compulsive disorder, and b) the elderly. I've been officially diagnosed that I belong in the first category, and with each passing day I march toward the latter.)

Honestly I don't know exactly why it is that I do this. But as I spent a good bit of yesterday's errands fiddling with these mirrors, I began to think about it. I have come to some ideas and maybe even some conclusions.

I believe that the reason I adjust my rear view mirrors so much is due to my obsession with the past. I'm constantly thinking about where I've already been. Indeed, rather than live in the present moment, I'm either living in (and regretting) my past or fearing what may come in the future. As we all know, this is a tragic waste of time and energy. In fact, it's one of the dumbest ways I can think of to spend one's time. Yet I do it—and I do it a good bit of the time it seems.

But in reading the quotes above, I think maybe I've been a little too hard on myself. Of course, the first one affirms my initial thoughts. But when I look at the second one, I see that there also can be a positive side to looking back. I think that for so long I have been looking back to find myself. You see, there was a time I thought of myself as a good person. There was a time I really liked myself. In looking back so much, I think I may be looking for that boy and young man I miss so much. And maybe that is not such a bad thing.

Over the last couple years, my "rear view looking" has brought much-needed change in me. As painful as they've been, my visitations with my past have brought changes in the right direction. I may still have a bit to go before I find myself in full measure, but I have hope. And as the character Andy Dufresne in The Shawshank Redemption reminds us, "hope is a good thing, maybe the best of things."

Looking too far back and too far forward can be a mistake. But done wisely, reviewing the past or planning for the future can be of help. Just as we do with our driving, the important thing is to look behind you or ahead with a positive purpose. Do anything else, and you might find yourself mired in no less than a catastrophe.

And remember; keep watch for those blind spots!

THE ART
OF BEING YOURSELF

"To be nobody but yourself in a world which is doing
its best, night and day, to make you everybody else
means to fight the hardest battle which any human
being can fight; and never stop fighting."

e. e. cummings

In the last chapter, I stated that probably the most important truth about finding peace and happiness is to live life in the present moment. Well, I will say that, along with that truth, there is another—and that is you simply must insist upon being yourself.

Life is full of pressure to be someone other than yourself. People are literally lined up to tell you how to look, what is true and what to believe in, how to act, what to like and dislike—it is never-ending. It's easy to become overwhelmed by all the demands.

Please don't make the same mistakes I have made. Don't buckle under the pressure and try to please everyone. Listen up—if you want any chance at all at peace and happiness, you have to be you. Period. And here's another thing—if certain people do not like who you are, you have to be able to simply say "so be it." That's just the gospel truth.

YOU DEFINE YOU

*"We must not allow other people's limited perceptions
to define us."*

Virginia Satir

*"Accept no one's definition of your life, but define
yourself."*

Harvey S. Firestone

We all tend to draw conclusions about one another. That's natural. But, sometimes, some of us take it too far. Some of us sum up or define a person by one or maybe a few characteristics. And the characteristics with which we define one another are broad—for example, we label each other sometimes by profession (doctor, lawyer, professional athlete), a religion (Jewish, Muslim, Buddhist), a sexual orientation or identity (gay, bisexual, transgender), or even a medical condition ("she suffers from Alzheimer's," "he is a depressive," or "she's dying of cancer"). I know this to be true because I've seen it many times in others—and sadly, I've seen it in myself.

We are too attached to these characteristics and tend to define one another by them. This is a mistake. Each of us is much more than one characteristic. In fact, we are much more than any number of characteristics. By defining others by their characteristics, while easy to do, this has the potential to limit us—sometimes in dangerous ways.

One example of this that comes to my mind is Francis Ford Coppola. If I were to ask you to describe this man, most of you would quickly state that he is a successful and respected filmmaker. This is true, but did you know that he also owns a wildly successful winery? You might if you drink wine. Did you also know that he owns a number of exclusive and exotic resorts and hotels? I'll bet most of you did not know that one. You see, Mr. Coppola is much more than a filmmaker. He's a very curious and driven man with lots of interests and lots of ambition. Like all of us, Francis Ford Coppola is made up of many things—thoughts, habits, characteristics and tastes.

Probably an even better example to make my point is Lou Gehrig. Playing all of 17 seasons for the New York Yankees, Gehrig set a number of records. He was nicknamed "The Iron Horse" for his durability. But, to some folks, he has sadly been reduced to being defined by a disease. Society even calls the ailment from which he suffered, ALS, as "Lou Gehrig's disease." What a disservice to such an accomplished individual.

My point here, obviously, is that we must all be careful with judgments based upon one or a few characteristics. Limiting someone to a stereotype based upon one or more characteristics never portrays a person accurately.

But the reason we must be so careful with this is that, sometimes, an individual who is labeled as something or other starts to see himself or herself as limited to that label. I know this was true of me for the longest time with depression. For years, I saw myself only as a person with depression. And because I accepted that characteristic as my defining one, others did, too. (I have since learned, thankfully, that I am not simply someone who has suffered from a terrible malady, but that I am much more.)

Let's please stop labeling each other. And, most importantly, let's please stop defining ourselves by others labels of us. Each one of us must define who we are ourselves. And we must strive to define ourselves in such a way that we are, or at least, become, proud of ourselves. Otherwise we die inside—simple as that.

Each one of us is no less than a human being. And each one of us is multi-faceted. Each of us is partly a reflection of our genetics. And each is partly a reflection of our experiences. But we are all so much more than any one or a few things. Accept no one's definition of yourself but your own. And then get up each morning and do what you need to do to live up to your own definition.

VALIDATION OF OTHERS

Have you ever stopped and asked yourself how many of your deeds or actions are done in seeking the validation of someone else or some group? Recently I was looking back over the Buddha's teaching of the Middle Way. Its main thrust is the avoidance of extremes. One of the Buddha's examples is the constant chasing after sense pleasures with include being possessed by "running after fame."

It has dawned on me many times that, while not exactly running after fame, one of the primary and enduring motivators in my life has been validation by others. Now, I don't mean the validation by close family members or friends. We obviously need close relationships with these individuals. Our family members and friends should be our most valued treasures.

No, I'm talking about validation from those who are outside this circle—even complete strangers. As a result of my own poor self-esteem or self-confidence, I often found myself at the mercy of others, and doing or not doing something based upon the perceived or real effect I may have on someone else.

Take this blog, for instance. While I am proud that I have always tried to speak from my heart, I am starting to find myself concerned with page view numbers, Facebook likes, and Twitter followers. This can easily turn into an obsession. And for what purpose? Really it's just to satisfy my own ego that others think that what I have to say is of some grand worth. And this should be the furthest thing from my mind. I need to get back to the days where the true joy came in the writing process and let the rest take care of itself. I'm losing some of that.

And so it is with the rest of my life. If my heart is a loving one, and if I seek goodness toward my fellow man, if I strive to always do the right thing, then that is really all that matters. I don't need to get caught up so much in the validation of others. What others think of me will vary from time to time. I will always find a group of folks who find me agreeable, and at least an equal number who will not. Okay, so what? Again, if my heart is focused on the right things, this is what matters in the end.

CHASING PERFECTION

"The more a human being feels himself a self, tries to intensify this self and reach a never-attainable perfection, the more drastically he steps out of the center of being."

Eugene Herrigel

"The courage to be is the courage to accept oneself, in spite of being unacceptable."

Paul Tillich

Chariots of Fire is one of my all-time favorite movies. This 1981 British film tells the (mostly) true story of the rivalry between two of the world's top sprinters—Harold Abrahams, and Englishman, and Eric Liddell, a Scotsman—competing in the 1924 Olympic Games. (The movie was nominated for seven Academy Awards and won four, including Best Picture.)

One of my favorite scenes comes early in the movie. During a pre-Olympic race, Liddell bests Abrahams by a razor-thin margin. Suffering his first ever loss, Abrahams is literally distraught beyond consolation. After the race, he's sitting in the stands; his pose is that of a little boy who's just been put in "time-out."

Seeking to console him, Abrahams' girlfriend, Sybil, comes to his side. "Harold," she says, "this is absolutely ridiculous. It's a race you've lost, not a relative. Nobody's dead." Abrahams replies, still in disbelief, "I lost." Then Sybil, "I know. I was there. I remember watching you; it was marvelous. You were marvelous. He was more marvelous, that's all. One that day the best man won . . . . He was ahead; there was nothing you could have done. He won fair and square." Then Abrahams, "Well, that's that." Sybil responds, "If you can't take a beating, perhaps it's for the best." Becoming angry, Abrahams shouts, "I don't run to take beatings—I run to win! If I can't win, I won't run." Sybil pauses, finally saying, "If you don't run, you can't win"

The movie portrays Liddell as a devout Christian running for the glory of God. Abrahams runs seemingly just to show the world he is the fastest man alive. Liddell pursues excellence, while Abrahams pursues perfection. And these two aims are worlds apart. The former will push you to achieve your best; the latter will destroy you.

One of my diagnoses includes that of OCD (Obsessive Compulsive Disorder). Many who suffer from OCD fall victim to pursuing perfection. At best, you are constantly frustrated at the imperfections of yourself and others. At worst, you are frozen from acting at all for fear you will not reach perfection. And though the OCD sufferer knows in his mind that perfection is impossible, his heart and soul won't let go of the notion. All this adds up to sustained misery.

We must realize that we are imperfect and live in an imperfect world. Moreover, society today pushes us to believe that perfection is something for which to strive. Excellence no longer seems good enough. No, it's perfection that impresses.

Look at Tiger Woods. (Forget his moral failing for a moment. These are, in my opinion, private matters between his family and him.) Let's look at Tiger Woods—golfer. These days all we hear about is Woods' "slump." Let me remind you that, at present, Woods (who is in year 15 of what could be a professional career lasting many more years) has already won 14 Majors (Jack Nicklaus holds the record with 18). At one time Woods held the position as the world's top golfer, which he held for a record number of weeks; he has been named PGA Player of the Year a record ten times (again, this in 15 seasons.) He is probably the most highly paid athlete on the planet and is worth literally hundreds of millions of dollars. Is this not excellence in athletics? Of course it is. Yet, what do we hear about today? Woods is slumping; he's in a hole. When will he get back to the old Woods? Someone, please show me this hole he's in. Not only that, someone please hurl me deep into this hole where, together, Woods and I can commiserate.

Pursuing perfection is futile. Please don't fall into this trap. Again, be yourself, and pursue personal excellence. Strive to be the best you can be and then let it go. Also, let the world be imperfect. Indeed, embrace this imperfect world as well—it's the only one we have.

The sooner we realize we are not perfect and the world is not perfect, the sooner we will become more accepting of ourselves and others, and the sooner we can get about the business of being ourselves and letting others be themselves. We just might learn to overlook imperfections in others and ourselves. And there is nothing quite so freeing than acceptance of whatever is.

Keep striving? Absolutely. It's your duty as a human being. You owe it to yourself and others—your family and friends. Pursue excellence and work hard toward it? Again, absolutely. But pursue perfection? It's a complete waste of time and a pursuit at which you will fail. No one is perfect. Accept that. Count your talents and blessings as the gifts they are. Do with them the best you can. But then, rest in the knowledge you have met your goals. Revel in the notion you are doing the best you can do and that should always be your goal—no less, but no more.

HATERS

"Hater: A person who simply cannot be happy for another's success. So rather than be happy they make a point of exposing a flaw in that person. Hating, the result of being a hater, is not exactly jealousy. The hater doesn't really want to be the person he or she hates, rather the hater wants to knock someone else down a notch."

Urban Dictionary

Years ago I wrote a book entitled Jazz Profiles: The Spirit of the Nineties. In the process of writing it, I interviewed many young and successful jazz artists. With one prominent artist, I raised the question of music critics and the role they play in the world of music. With that question, I certainly hit his hot button. He summed up the critic this way—"What is a critic? A critic is someone who makes judgments on what someone else is doing without ever having to do anything himself. I mean, what a job to have!" In the editing process, the exchange was removed at the request of his publicist.

This exchange made a lasting impression on me. I won't ever forget it. What a true statement! And since our conversation, I have regularly noticed the number of critics and haters in this world. Why do I bring up this topic? Because, in finding and being your true self, I want you to be aware of the hater and also learn to take him or her for what he or she is—a hater—and that is all he or she is, absolutely nothing more. And once you identify a hater, my advice is to stay as far away as you can.

Like the music critic, in my opinion the hater really has nothing positive or substantive to offer. Haters, due to their own low self-esteem, simply have taken on the only role they can find for themselves—criticizing others. And the hater will criticize virtually anything—from outward appearances (tattoos, piercings, hairstyles, choice of clothing) to any religion not of their own, to sexual identity, even to simply any thoughts or opinions that are not of their own.

Haters are especially dangerous to those who are attempting to think for themselves and discover and be their true selves. For one thing, haters are generally very vocal, even loud, in their criticism. And despite the shaky premises on which they base their drivel, haters are sometimes many in numbers. History teaches us this. For example, as much as we all now see the ignorance and destructive nature of racial prejudice, at on time there were many who denounced those of a different race from their own. The same has been true for those who criticize the LGBT community or religions about which the haters know virtually nothing. In general, haters of any kind base criticism on one thing and one thing only—they somehow feel threatened by anything that is different from their own way or view.

In discovering and becoming yourself, you must do two things. First, you must realize that haters are and will remain out there. Unfortunately this is not going to change. Second, you must muster the courage to see the hater for what he or she is and not allow the criticism to change you. For if you do, the hater will accomplish his or her goal—that of destroying your creativity, destroying your true identity, and in making you feel inferior. If you are committed to being yourself, you must be strong enough to face this.

But there is a silver lining—for haters are just like bullies. Their strength lies only in bluff and in numbers. Stand up to a hater and you will see he or she really has no true strength at all. The hater is solely huff and puff. If you can muster the courage to stand your ground, usually the hater will run and hide, only to come out again to prey upon one who won't stand up.

In becoming and embracing one's true self, one has to endure the pain of dealing with critics and haters. And as difficult and painful as it can be, I want you to know that standing your ground is worth the effort. And I want you to know that you can get through the hating process and come out better on the other side.

Be strong. Be yourself. And stand up to your haters in the wisest way—with calm and peaceful resistance to join their weak ways. Learn to love and smile at your haters. They need kindness and compassion just like everyone else. Meeting hate with hate accomplishes nothing you are after. Also, doing so only makes you one of them. And we want to avoid this at all costs.

Arm yourself with love, kindness, and compassion to meet any resistance you may encounter. Be ready—be ready with love in your heart. There is nothing quite so powerful as love.

MY BERRY PICKING DAYS ARE OVER

"The primary joy of life is acceptance, approval, the sense of appreciation and companionship of our human comrades. Many men do not understand that the need for fellowship is really as deep as the need for food, and so they go through life accepting many substitutes for the genuine, warm, simple."
Joshua Loth Liebman

My mother's family was a farming family from Kentucky. My grandfather was primarily a dairy farmer, but the family was pretty much self-sufficient. They literally raised or grew almost everything they had for meals—from all types of meats and fish, to all their vegetables and fruits. Fact is, they lived like a lot of folks growing up in rural Kentucky through the Depression era and until many years later.

As a young lady, my mother married, and she and my dad started their own family. But we really hadn't moved all that far from the farm of her childhood—only a couple hours away to a small town called Hopkinsville. We visited my grandparents often—especially in the summer—and some of my fondest memories about growing up are of the trips back to that farm.

Every summer, we'd devote a good portion of one day to picking blackberries. (My grandmother made wonderful blackberry cobbler. I can still see her pouring all that sugar over the berries—sweetening them to perfection.)

As a little boy, I was allowed to go and bring along my own basket. I tried to pick good berries, but try as I did, most of mine were ultimately rejected as unworthy of cobbler. (Mine were always not yet ripe, too small, sour—you name it, something was usually wrong with my chosen berries.) After an hour or so, the sun would become too hot for me and I would abandon the whole project and go find my grandfather—hanging with him was always more interesting anyway.

Lately, I've been thinking a lot about my—really, everyone's—need to accept everyone else just the way they are. Unlike blackberries, the goal with people should not be to accept only the most mature, most pleasant, sweetest of the lot. We must learn to take the approach I did with my own blackberry picking as a child—we should accept one and all.

This approach is the best one for a couple reasons. First we are all unique. We all have strengths, faults, endearing traits and ones not so much. But, as human beings, we are all of equal value. Unlike blackberries, each human being is just as worthy of acceptance as the next.

Secondly, it is simply much easier to accept everyone than to pick and choose. Here's where my theory on blackberry picking works best—with humans. If we can ever just learn to accept all our brothers and sisters (no matter whether they are pleasant or not, wealthy or not, healthy or not, accept us in return or not), believe me, our whole lives would become much easier. You see, if we used the approach I used for berry picking, we wouldn't have to waste time judging and deciding who is worthy and who is not. We'd simply accept (and even learn to love) everyone. Let me repeat myself—we must accept, and even learn to love, everyone!

Please, let's not mistake our fellow human beings for blackberries. We all need and deserve acceptance, love, and compassion from everyone else. And if we could ever learn to give that acceptance, love, and compassion to all, life would be much more pleasant for us all—and also much easier. And that is a simple truth.

BE YOURSELF, BE BEAUTIFUL

"Make the most of yourself, for that is all there is of you."
Ralph Waldo Emerson

Recently, I picked up a copy of Shambhala Sun magazine. (Its cover photo and article featured Thich Nhat Hanh, so I couldn't resist.) The article (including an extensive interview) is wonderful, and I recommend it to you. (January 2012 Edition.)

What struck me the most was one simple sentence, "So anything you do for yourself, you do for the world." I thought to myself that those eleven words make up absolutely everything both FindMyOwnCurrent.com and fromi2us.com are about.

Being your best self always benefits you personally. I think that is obvious to everyone. But Nhat Hanh is also reminding us that being your best self benefits no less than the entire world as well. Being your best self provides an example to others, provides a benefit to the environment, and, most importantly, allows the entire world to experience the benefit of having you be a part. There is only one you. And there will only be one you—ever. Do us all a favor and bring your best every single day. Leave your mark—show us what you got!

Please, let yourself shine. We all need you.

IT'S INSIDE THE SOUL

"You have to grow from the inside out. None can teach you, none can make you spiritual. There is no other teacher but your own soul."
										Swami Vivekananda

"The soul becomes dyed with the color of its thoughts."
										Marcus Aurelius

The quality I admire most in a person is a genuine aura of goodness. With those who have it, you notice it immediately. The eyes give it away—the eyes are always smiling brightly.

This "goodness vibe," while manifesting itself on the outside, stems from one's soul. We all have at least some measure of this—it's deep inside every one of us. But there are those who nurture and grow theirs to the point it literally bursts out and becomes part of their appearance.

I wish I had this quality. I really do. Maybe one day I will, although I clearly do not at this time. But the good news for me is that I know where and how to acquire the full measure of it.

The answer lies in the two quotes above. The first reminds us that we are our best teacher. We inherently know what is good, what is right, what is best. It's true, goodness cannot really be taught by one to another. But there's no need to worry—our teacher is right inside us.

The second quote states one of the most important truths I know. Clearly we are the product of our thoughts. Honestly, we don't even have a choice in the matter. If we fill our minds and hearts with the ugly and repugnant, we become ugly and repugnant. However, the converse it also true. If we fill our minds and hearts with peace and goodness, we become and will emit these qualities as well.

It would do us all a world of good to take a meaningful look at ourselves. We need to think about the vibes we are producing on a consistent basis. If we are not proud of the energy we release, then we need to get about working on our thoughts. We need to properly nurture our minds and our hearts.

I, for one, have a lot of work ahead of me. But, thankfully, I at least know where to turn my attention.

AFTERWORD

I'm blessed. I am blessed with that wonderful feeling when you feel you have finally crossed over—crossed over a hurdle you thought for so long was too hard to conquer. I made it home—home to myself—and I'm never looking back.

As I mentioned, this book is a line of demarcation for me. It is Thursday, June 14, 2012 as I type this Afterword. I know my life will never be the same again. Writing this book has meant that much to me. I will walk as a different person now. (If you see me backsliding, you let me know—in a gentle way.)

Don't get me wrong. I still have much work to do. I'm reminded of the questions Liz Murray asked herself—if I really commit to change, and then give my all to making those changes a reality, can I really succeed? Honestly, only time will tell, but I know I'm on the right track.

Truth is, we all are walking up Lombard. Some of us see only the steep terrain, the sharp twists and turns, and fret about the inevitable obstacles along the way. The wise, however, focus their attention on the beauty. And the wise know this makes the climb worthwhile.

I hope you all find your authentic self and I hope you will live your own life. I hope you all find peace, joy, and happiness in your hearts. Remember, we are all persons of consequence. And there is nothing more valuable than to get about the business of living a life of consequence—for others and, not the least of which, for yourself. I will be wishing you all the best on your journey.

Peace to you all.

RLC

MY DEEPEST LONGING

"In the end we shall have had enough of cynicism and skepticism and humbug and we shall want to live more musically."

Vincent van Gogh

For the longest time, one could use any one of three words to sum me up succinctly—cynical, skeptical, or negative. I am ashamed of this, but I know it to be the truth.

But I know I have changed—changed a lot. (Truth is, however, a lot of folks haven't noticed and honestly couldn't care less. You see, most folks I used to see on a regular basis are no longer in my life. Those I see regularly now didn't know the old me. And for the most part, those familiar with both the old and new me are simply "over" the whole issue. Almost everyone has a point at which they simply "tune out" someone with persistent problems with depression and such.)

You know what? I'm tired of the old me, too. I'm not tired of living—just tired of living as I have for so long. I'm tired of being a cynic, a skeptic, and a negative person. So, what do I do? How do I change my basic nature and personality?

Well, I have a plan. I am going to embark on the most daring of experiments—a very naïve experiment, perhaps. Through prayer, meditation, and sheer willpower, I'm setting about to make a complete change—to develop into an open, positive, and cheerful human being—not a sappy sweet kind of cheerful, mind you, just uncommonly pleasant. (I can't believe I just typed this! It's difficult for me to believe that I actually have reached a point where I want to live, as van Gogh put it, more musically.)

As beautiful as all this sounds to me, however, the victory (if reached) will be bittersweet. For I wish those who knew the difficult and negative me could see the new me. And I really wish those who are familiar with both really cared about the transformation. Yes, it's very un-Buddha of me, but I am still attached to the notion that those who knew or know me would really see me—again, see and acknowledge the progress I've made.

But I can't worry about all this now. I suppose maybe that I will never get there if one of my goals is that others see me get there. I must focus on what's important—just getting there. I must focus on becoming open, caring, one who gives folks a chance, one who doesn't meet others with pre-judgment. I must focus on doing away with the humbug. I must now live musically.

I owe this final change to many—to my immediate family, to those with whom I am in regular contact, to my extended family, and to myself. Also, and most importantly, I owe this to God—He created me and I need to get about the business of making Him proud.

This is the most exciting (and most difficult) undertaking I've ever begun. As we all have, I've taken on many challenges in my life. But this one is, for me, "big time" big. And failing is not an option.

Yes, I want to live musically. When you see me, I want you to see something out of the ordinary. I want my appearance to be fey. But even more so, I want my inner being to be fey—when I walk down the street, I want folks to hear Mozart. I want to sound like the beautiful cello playing of Yo-Yo Ma. I want to be as graceful as Baryshnikov.

You know, it's almost embarrassing to put this in print. But I want to be able to look back one day and say, "I did it." I turned things around completely." Time will tell.

BEING QUIET

*"A happy life must be to a great extent a quiet life, for
it is only in an atmosphere of quiet that
true joy dare live."*

Bertrand Russell

Twenty-eight years ago today, February 13, 1984, my
father (at age 46) had a fatal heart attack. Ever since, this day
has obviously been significant for me. I had a special dad, and so
February 13 is a special day for me. These days, it's been not so
sad as it once was, but it's still significant.

Every year at this time, I think about what my dad would think
of me and where I am in my life's journey. It's been a long time since
I thought this way, but this year I think my dad would be proud of
me. He would know now that I am for real. He would know that
these days, I'm at least headed in the right direction.

My dad was all about what is real. He was the very antithesis
of being pretentious. He loathed anything or anybody who wasn't
for real. Long before it was popular among males, my dad chose
to be a nurse, and he cared deeply about people—deep inside the
hearts and souls of people.

Every year since he died, I've tried to talk with him. Most years
he has not answered. But, he did this year. I said, "what's up?" He
said, "Reg, be quiet now. You have said enough. Try listening—it
will work better for you. Just let it all be." My dad spoke this year
and that is what he said.

And you know what? I know what he meant. I have said enough. I've talked enough. It's time to listen. And so, now I will listen. I'm excited about just listening. Maybe I will learn the rest of what I need to learn. I don't know. I'm not as wise as my dad. But this year he says I'm ready to try.

So I will do less preaching. I will do more observing. I will do less judging. I will do more praising. I will "back off" as I don't know near what I think I know. (This is what Pops was trying in his nice way to say.)

My dad, he was so cool—the coolest. And he is still teaching me—he's always teaching me. So, I'm all about just trying to listen and learn now. In the quiet, I want to listen. I want the quiet to land on my face—just like snow. I want the quiet to land on my face the way it landed on Pops' face.

I want to speak sparingly, but wisely. I want to be the person Pops would be proud of. And that person would be more loving, more gentle, a lot kinder, and a lot wiser. That person would be his son—as I know I can be.